THE BRITISH
QUESTION BOOK

TONY BUSHELL   DAVID WAUGH

Nelson

Thomas Nelson and Sons Ltd
Nelson House Mayfield Road
Walton-on-Thames Surrey
KT12 5PL UK

51 York Place
Edinburgh
EH1 3JD UK

Thomas Nelson (Hong Kong) Ltd
Toppan Building 10/F
22A Westlands Road
Quarry Bay Hong Kong

Thomas Nelson Australia
102 Dodds Street
South Melbourne
Victoria 3205 Australia

Nelson Canada
1120 Birchmount Road
Scarborough Ontario
M1K 5G4 Canada

© David Waugh and Tony Bushell 1991
First published by Thomas Nelson and Sons Ltd 1991

ISBN 0-17-434291-8

NPN 9 8 7 6 5 4 3 2 1

All rights reserved. No paragraph of this publication may be reproduced, copied or transmitted save with written permission or in accordance with the provisions of the Copyright, Design and Patents Act 1988, or under the terms of any licence permitting limited copying issued by the Copyright Licensing Agency, 33-34 Alfred Place, London WC1E 7DP.

Any person who does any unauthorised act in relation to this publication may be liable to criminal prosecution and civil claims for damages.

Printed and bound in Hong Kong

The publishers are grateful to the following for permission to reproduce photographs and copyright material:

London East Anglian Group; Midland Examining Group; Northern Examining Association, (Associated Lancashire Schools Examining Board, Joint Matriculation Board, North Regional Examinations Board, North West Regional Examination Board, Yorkshire and Humberside Regional Examinations Board); Southern Examining Group; Hunting Aerofilms: p.57; David Waugh: p.16, p.44; Welsh Development Agency: p.39.
The Ordnance Survey Map on pages 76-77 is reproduced from the Ordnance Survey 1:50,000 Landranger Map with permission of the controller of Her Majesty's Stationery Office © Crown Copyright.

CONTENTS

1	**LAND AND PEOPLE**	4
2	**CLIMATE AND PEOPLE**	8
3	**FARMING AND CHANGE**	12
4	**FORESTRY AND LANDSCAPE**	18
5	**WATER — SUPPLY AND DEMAND**	20
6	**ENERGY — SUPPLY AND DEMAND**	26
7	**INDUSTRY AND CHANGE**	32
8	**RESIDENTIAL ENVIRONMENTS**	40
9	**POPULATION CHANGES**	48
10	**TRANSPORT**	54
11	**SHOPPING**	58
12	**RECREATION AND TOURISM**	64
13	**COMPETITION FOR LAND**	68
14	**ENVIRONMENTAL ISSUES**	72
15	**POLITICAL DECISIONS**	74
16	**THE SEA**	80

ONE LAND AND PEOPLE

1 Refer to page 4 in the resource book. Study Figure 1a below which shows a partly completed drainage basin system.

a i) Make a copy of Figure 1a.
  ii) Describe how a drainage system works by writing the following terms in the boxes numbered 1 to 7: **evaporation groundwater infiltration interception surface run-off throughflow transpiration**.
(7 marks)

b Using your completed diagram:
  i) Name one input into the system.
  ii) Name three outputs from the system.
  iii) Give two ways in which water may be stored within the system.
  iv) Give three ways by which water may be transferred within the system.
  v) Which of the three methods you named in part iv) transfers water the most quickly to the river?
(12 marks)

c What is the difference between:
  i) evaporation and transpiration,
  ii) infiltration and interception,
  iii) surface run-off and throughflow?
(6 marks)

d How would the following situations change the drainage basin system:
  i) the ground being frozen in winter,
  ii) the rock and soil being impermeable?
(2 marks)

Figure 1a

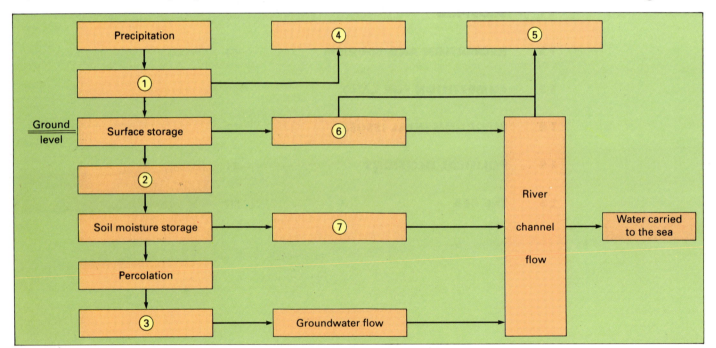

2 Refer to Figure 1.4 on page 5 of the resource book.

a i) Using Figure 1.4, state how run-off in winter differs from that in summer.
  ii) Suggest reasons for your answer in **a** i).
  iii) Give two factors, other than rainfall, which can affect the amount of run-off.
(11 marks)

b Using the information in Figure 1.4 suggest why a reservoir might be built in this drainage basin.
(2 marks)

LEAG A, 1988

LAND AND PEOPLE

3 Study Figure 1b which gives information about rainfall and discharge of a stream flowing over an impermeable rock on 5th October 1987.

Figure 1b

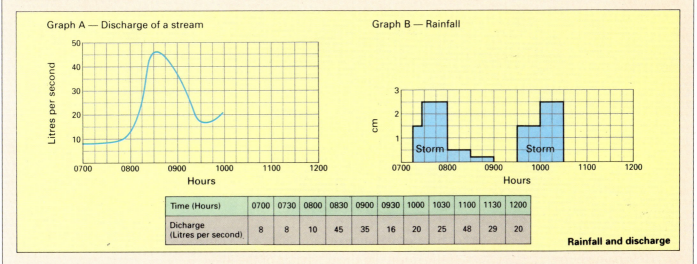

Rainfall and discharge

a i) What is meant by an impermeable rock?
  ii) Give an example of 'an impermeable rock'. (2 marks)

b i) Copy and complete Graph A using the figures given in the table.
  ii) When did Storm 1 start? (3 marks)

c i) What is meant by the 'discharge' of a stream?
  ii) What was the time lag between the start of Storm 1 and the first peak in stream discharge?
  iii) Suggest three reasons why there was a lag time. (5 marks)

LEAG, B 1988

4 Refer to page 6 in the resource book. Study Figure 1c which shows two different storm hydrographs.

Figure 1c

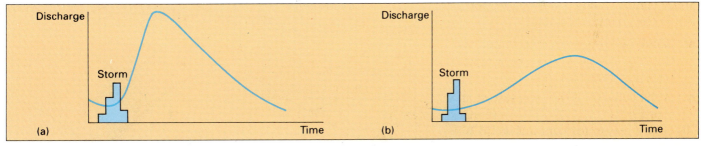

The following incomplete table gives several reasons for the different shapes of the two hydrographs.

a Copy out the table filling in the missing parts (Figure 1d). (5 marks)

b Give a reason for the differences in the two hydrographs. (5 marks)

	Hydrograph A	Hydrograph B	Reason
Intensity of rain		Gentle rain over a lengthy period	
Rock/soil type		Porous/chalk	
Vegetation	Very little. No leaves on trees		
Previous weather	Very wet		
Temperature	Very cold (winter) Very hot (summer)		

Figure 1d

LAND AND PEOPLE

5 Refer to the diagram and graphs in Figure 1e.   **Figure 1e**

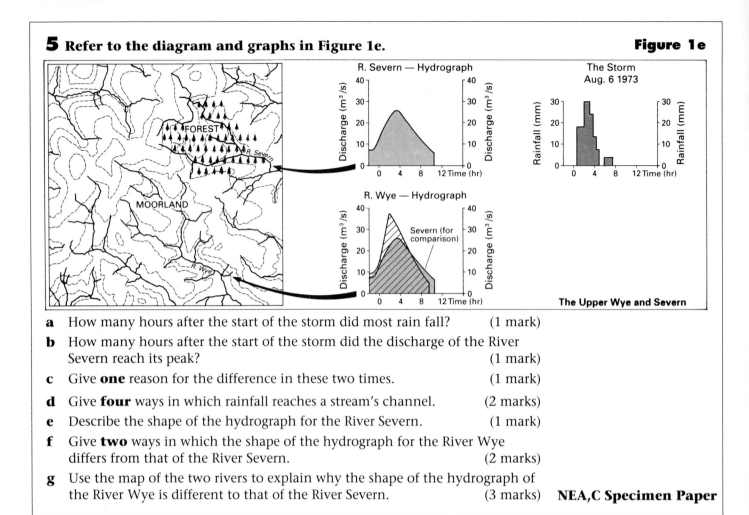

The Upper Wye and Severn

a How many hours after the start of the storm did most rain fall? (1 mark)

b How many hours after the start of the storm did the discharge of the River Severn reach its peak? (1 mark)

c Give **one** reason for the difference in these two times. (1 mark)

d Give **four** ways in which rainfall reaches a stream's channel. (2 marks)

e Describe the shape of the hydrograph for the River Severn. (1 mark)

f Give **two** ways in which the shape of the hydrograph for the River Wye differs from that of the River Severn. (2 marks)

g Use the map of the two rivers to explain why the shape of the hydrograph of the River Wye is different to that of the River Severn. (3 marks)

NEA,C Specimen Paper

6 Page 7 of the resource book will help you to answer this question.

Study Figure 1f which shows a section across the channel of a river.

Figure 1f

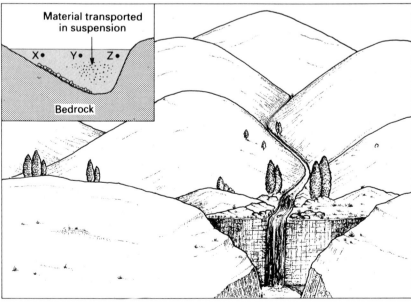

a Name two processes, not named on the diagram, by which a river may transport material.

b i) Is the velocity of the river fastest at X, Y or Z? (2 marks)

ii) Give a reason for your answer to **b** i). (2 marks)

c At which of the three points X, Y or Z will:

i) erosion be greatest,

ii) deposition occur? (2 marks)

d Name three processes by which a river may erode its banks and bed. (3 marks)

7 Page 7 of the resource book will help you to answer this question.   **Figure 1g**

Copy Figure 1g which is a landsketch of the upper course of a river valley. On it label the following:

V-shaped valley   interlocking spurs   rapids   waterfall   plunge pool

LAND AND PEOPLE

8 Refer to pages 8 and 9 in the resource book.
a In what ways may rivers prove to be an advantage to:
   i) farmers,   ii) industrialists,   iii) tourists? (6 marks)
b How may rivers be polluted by:
   i) farmers,   ii) industrialists,   iii) tourists? (6 marks)
c Study Figure 1.12 on page 9 of the resource book which shows the 'clean up' of the River Tyne. It shows water quality to be divided into four classes — A, B, C and D.
   i) Which of the four classes provides water which is safe enough to drink without extensive treatment?
   ii) In which of the four classes can fish live comfortably? (2 marks)

The River Tyne at Ryton is 30 km from the sea.
   iii) How many of these 30 km were heavily polluted in 1975?
   iv) How many of these 30 km were heavily polluted in 1985?
   v) Why was there less heavy pollution in 1985 than in 1975? (3 marks)

9 Refer to Page 10 in the resource book.
Copy and complete Figure 1h.
The words across show ways in which people may use coasts. The words down are problems resulting from the use of coasts. (Figures in brackets show the number of letters per word.)

Figure 1h

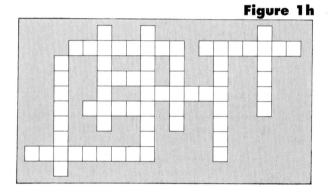

Across sand (4)   hotel (5)   stacks (6)
            tourism (7)   caravans (8)   sand dunes (9)

Down   litter (6)   sewage (6)   erosion (7)
            oilslick (8)   effluent (8)   landslips (9)

10 Refer to page 11 in the resource book.
Study Figure 1i which shows a glacial system.

Figure 1i

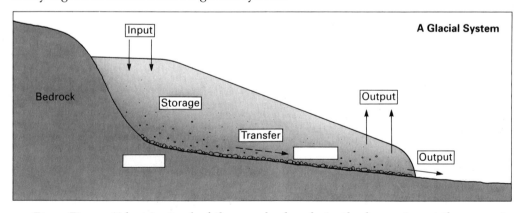

a Draw Figure 1i but instead of the words already in the boxes insert the correct ones from the following list:

evaporation   glacier   ice   meltwater   snow

b Write in the two correct empty boxes, the words **ablation** and **accumulation**.
c What might lead to an increase in
   i) glacial inputs   ii) glacial outputs? (2 marks)
d What will happen to the glacier if there is an increase in
   i) inputs,   ii) outputs? (2 marks)

TWO CLIMATE AND PEOPLE

1 Figure 2a below shows average temperatures (°C) in Britain in July (reduced to sea level).

Figure 2a

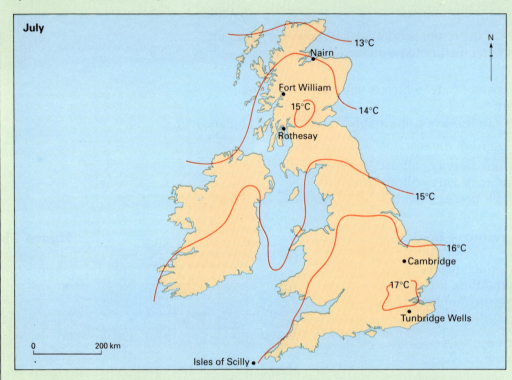

i) Complete the paragraph below by crossing out the incorrect words:

Nairn has a temperature in July of (15°/14°C) while the warmest place in England is (the Isles of Scilly/London). This shows that temperatures (increase/decrease) from south to north. The lines of equal temperature are called (contours/isotherms) and they run from (north to south/east to west). The 15°C temperature loops (southwards/northwards) over the Irish Sea. This shows the land to be (cooler/warmer) than the sea in summer. (7 marks)

ii) Explain the difference in land and sea temperatures in the summer time. (4 marks)

b Figure 2b below shows a mountain range with rain-bearing winds coming from the east.

Figure 2b

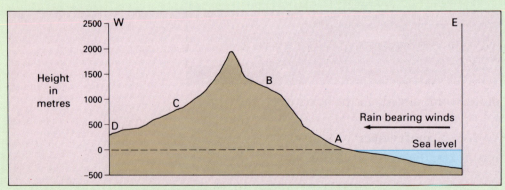

i) Which of the four locations, A, B, C or D, is likely to receive the heaviest rainfall?

ii) Give reasons for your answer. (3 marks)

LEAG, 1988

CLIMATE AND PEOPLE

2 Refer to page 12 in the resource book. Copy Figure 2c and complete it by placing the following words in the correct spaces:

over 2000 mm   under 2000 mm;   cereals;   sheep;   water deficit; water surplus. **(6 marks)**

Figure 2c

	Wales and West Scotland	Eastern England
Amount of rain		
Type of farming		
Water supply		

3 Refer to Figure 2.2 on page 12 of the resource book.

a i) What is the January average rainfall for Fort William?
 ii) Which season of the year (Spring, Summer, Autumn or Winter) has the highest rainfall in Fort William?
 iii) Which place, Penzance or Margate, has the higher average annual rainfall?
 iv) Give one reason for your answer to **a** iii).
 v) Give one reason why, of the four places, Fort William receives the most annual rainfall. **(5 marks)**

b i) What is the maximum temperature for Fort William?
 ii) What is the minimum temperature for Fort William?
 iii) What is the annual range of temperature for Fort William?
 iv) Give **one** reason why Margate is warmer than Aberdeen in summer.
 v) Give **one** reason why Penzance is warmer than Margate in winter.
 vi) Which place, Aberdeen or Margate, is likely to have the greater rate of evaporation in summer? **(6 marks)**

4 Pages 12-13 in the resource book may help you to answer this question.
Look at Figure 2d. Choose four groups of people from each season.
For each group describe the type of weather they might prefer during that season.
In each case give a reason for your answer. **(8 marks)**

Figure 2d

Group A in winter	Group B in summer
Ski-instructor	Ice-cream seller
Farmer producing early vegetables	Wimbledon tennis player
Plumber	Forestry worker
Double glazing salesperson	Strawberry grower
An elderly person	A dairy farmer
Long distance lorry driver	Fair-skinned person

5 Refer to page 14 in the resource book. Aberfan was the worst disaster of its kind in Great Britain.

a i) What type of movement caused the disaster?
 ii) Which industrial activity led to the building of the tip?
 iii) What advance warning of the disaster occurred in 1944?
 iv) Give **two** pieces of evidence to show that the disaster was partly due to natural causes.
 v) Give **two** pieces of evidence to show that the disaster was partly due to human mismanagement. **(7 marks)**

b What was the immediate effect of the disaster? **(2 marks)**

c What steps do you think were taken after 1966 to make sure that a similar disaster would never occur again? **(2 marks)**

6 Refer to page 15 in the resource book and study Figure 2e which shows a sketch plan of a drainage basin in Cumbria.

Figure 2e

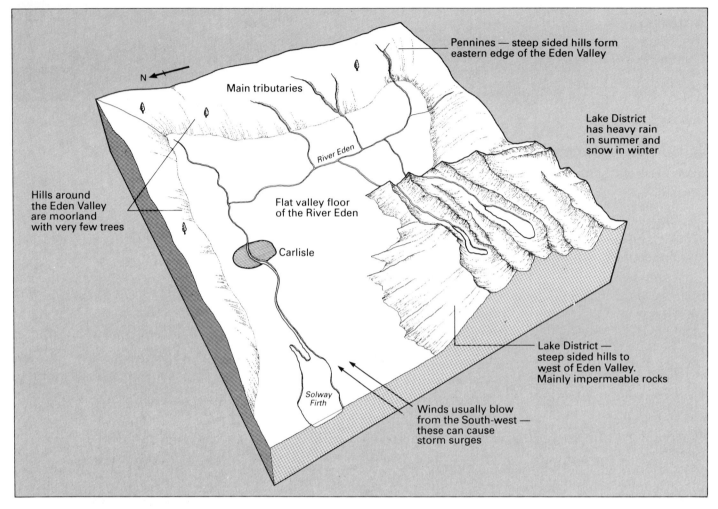

a i) Name the river which flows through Carlisle.
  ii) Name **two** highland areas where tributaries to this river rise. (3 marks)

b Give **three** reasons why there is always a risk of flooding in the Carlisle area. (3 marks)

c How did the following factors contribute to this particular flood.
  i) rising temperatures,
  ii) rainfall,
  iii) strong winds,
  iv) the spring tide? (4 marks)

d Give **three** effects which the flood had on the people living near to the river. (3 marks)

e What attempts have been made since the flood to try to prevent a future recurrence? (3 marks)

7 Refer to pages 16 and 17 in the resource book.
Imagine that you are a newswriter for your local television station. You are told that **either** a severe gale, a heavy snowfall, a severe frost **or** a dense fog is expected in the next few hours.
Write a **brief** warning notice, to be read out on television, to ensure that viewers listen and take any necessary precautions. (4 marks)

CLIMATE AND PEOPLE

8 Refer to page 15 in the resource book which gives information about the drought of 1975-76.

a What was the weather like in:
  i) the summer of 1975,
  ii) the winter of 1975-76,
  iii) the summer of 1976? (3 marks)

b i) Why did so little rain fall during this period of time?
  ii) Which parts of England and Wales received less than 59% of their annual rainfall totals?
  iii) Which part of England and Wales was least affected by the drought? (5 marks)

c i) Name **three** cities which had water rationing.
  ii) Name **two** other methods used to try to restrict the use of water. (5 marks)

e How did the drought affect the following groups of people:
  i) householders,
  ii) farmers,
  iii) industrialists,
  iv) forestry workers. (4 marks)

f Name **two** groups of people who might have benefitted from the drought. (2 marks)

9 Study Figure 2f which shows details of Britain's worst storm in October 1987 (adapted from newspaper reports of that time).

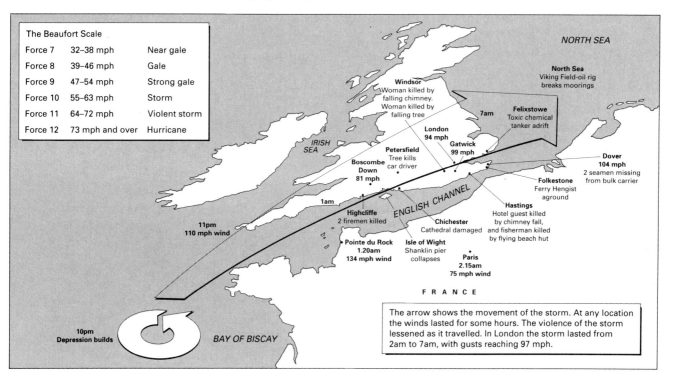

  i) From Figure 2f, state which location received the strongest winds. (1 mark)
  ii) According to the Beaufort Scale, what force of wind was recorded at London? (1 mark)
  iii) How long did the gale last in London? (1 mark)
  iv) Using the information from Figure 2f, describe how the people of Southern England were affected by the storm. (4 marks)

Figure 2f

NEA, C 1989

THREE FARMING AND CHANGE

1 Refer to page 18 of the resource book as well as using your own background knowledge.

a Are farms in Britain found in urban or rural areas? (1 mark)

b What is meant by **each** of the following three types of farming: **arable**, **pastoral** and **mixed**? (3 marks)

Read the paragraph headed 'Farming has become an essential industry'.

c Name **two** machines which save the farmer time and eliminate back breaking jobs. (2 marks)

d The modern buildings on some farms include broiler sheds and dairy parlours.
  i) Name the type of animal kept in each building. (2 marks)
  ii) Name a product which each animal provides for the farmer to sell. (2 marks)
  iii) What are the advantages to the farmer of keeping his animals in either a broiler shed or a milking parlour? (2 marks)
  iv) Why do many people dislike this modern method of farming? (2 marks)

2 Use Figure 3a and pages 18 and 19 in the resource book.

a i) How many farm workers were there in 1935?
  ii) What has happened to the number of farmworkers since then?
  iii) What other information shown on the graph helps to explain your answer to ii)?
  iv) Describe the changes in the number of horses on the farm.
  v) Give a reason for the changes you have described. (5 marks)

b Study the cartoon below concerning EC agriculture (Figure 3b).
  i) What EC problem does the cartoon suggest to you?
  ii) Using your knowledge and the information shown in the cartoon explain how the problem has arisen.
  iii) One solution to the problem in the United Kingdom recently considered is to 'sell off' unwanted farmland. State how this might help. (7 marks)

NEA, D 1988

Figure 3a

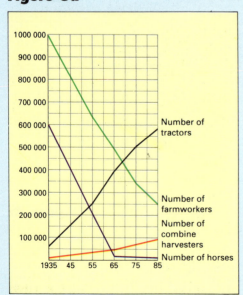

Figure 3b

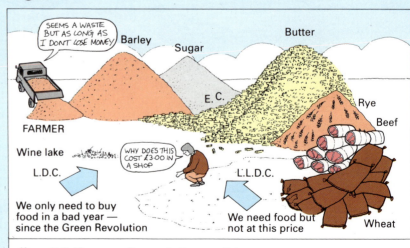

Key E.C. (European Economic Community)
     L.D.C. (Less Developed Countries)
     L.L.D.C. (Least Less Developed Countries)

FARMING AND CHANGE

3 Refer to Figure 3.4 on page 18 in the resource book.

a i) Name **two** regions which have over 4.1% of their workforce employed in agriculture. (2 marks)

ii) Name the **two** regions which have less than 1.0% of their workforce employed in agriculture. (2 marks)

iii) What percentage of the workforce in Scotland is employed in agriculture? (1 mark)

b Why are so few people in Britain employed in agriculture? (2 marks)

4 The sketches below (Figure 3c) compare farming 50 years ago and at present.

Figure 3c

1930s

1980s

a State **one** difference, shown on the sketches, between farming in the 1930s and the 1980s under each of the following headings.
 i) Field size.
 ii) Farm size. (2 marks)

b State **two** other differences, shown on the sketches, between farming in the 1930s and the 1980s. (2 marks)

c Explain why the field size has changed between the 1930s and the 1980s. (1 mark)

d Why have some people opposed this change? (1 mark)

NEA,B 1988

FARMING AND CHANGE

5 Study the maps below (Figure 3d) which show the same farm at different times.

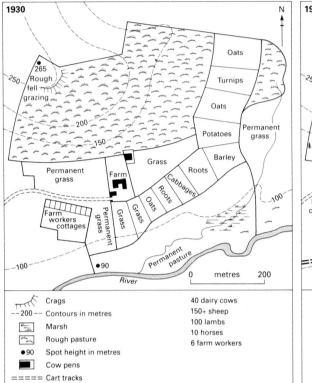

Figure 3d

i) What are the highest and lowest points on the farm? (2 marks)
ii) Describe the relief of the area shown on the map. (2 marks)
iii) The table below (Figure 3e) shows the approximate percentages of land uses on the farm in 1930 and 1984.

Land use	1930 %	1984 %
Grazing including rough pasture, permanent and sown grass	72	50
Cereals (barley and oats)	10	25
Root crops	10	5
Forestry	0	15
Others	8	5

Figure 3e

The figures for 1930 are plotted on the bar graph below (Figure 3f). In the spaces provided draw a similar graph to show the 1984 figures. (5 marks)

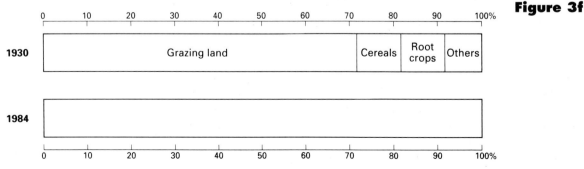

Figure 3f

iv) Describe two changes in land use which have occurred on the farm between 1930 and 1984. (2 marks)

MEG/WJEC, E 1988

FARMING AND CHANGE

6 Refer again to the two maps given in Question 5 and also to Figure 3.13 on page 23 of the resource book.

a Three types of land use shown on the maps in Question 5 are marsh, rough pasture and coniferous plantation.
 i) Which type was present in 1930 but not in 1984?
 ii) Which type was present in 1984 but not in 1930?
 iii) Which type was present in both 1930 and 1984? (3 marks)

b i) Why is the area next to the river left as permanent grass? (1 mark)
 ii) Are cereals grown under 100 metres; between 100 and 150 metres or over 150 metres? (1 mark)
 iii) Is the coniferous plantation on high or low land; flat or steep land; good quality or poor quality farmland? (3 marks)
 iv) Give one reason for your answers in part **b** iii). (1 mark)

c What reason can you suggest for:
 i) dairy cows being reared on the farm in 1930 but not in 1984, (1 mark)
 ii) horses being kept on the farm in 1930 but not in 1984,
 iii) more sheep and lambs being reared in 1984 than in 1930? (3 marks)

d Many farmers are turning to tourism as a second source of income. Using Figure 3d or Figure 3.13, map B on page 23 of the resource book:
 i) Name the **two** types of accommodation available to tourists.
 ii) Name the animal which may be used by tourists. (3 marks)

7 With reference to pages 21 and 24 in the resource book, complete the following diagram (Figure 3g) to show how the farming system applies to an arable farm in East Anglia. (10 marks)

Figure 3g

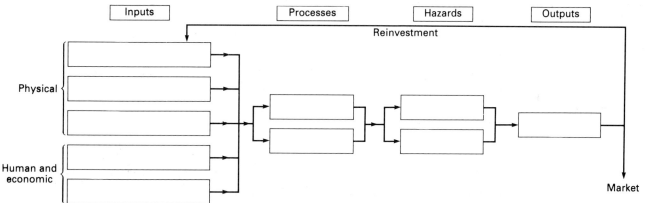

8 Refer to Figure 3.10 on page 21 of the resource book.

a In relation to the farming system, what is meant by each of the following terms: 'inputs', 'processes' and 'outputs'? (3 marks)

b With reference to a dairy farm:
 i) Name **three** physical inputs (3 marks)
 ii) Name **three** human and economic inputs. (3 marks)
 iii) Name **two** inputs which may vary from year to year. (2 marks)
 iv) Name **two** processes which take part on the farm. (2 marks)
 v) Name **two** outputs from the farm. (2 marks)
 vi) Why is it important that the value of the outputs should exceed the costs of the inputs? (1 mark)
 vii) Why should the farmer reinvest some of any surplus money? (1 mark)
 viii) Name two hazards which might affect a dairy farm. (2 marks)

FARMING AND CHANGE

9 Refer to Figure 3.6 in the resource book.

a Figure 3h opposite shows five different types of farming found in the British Isles. Rearrange the letters to name these five farming types. (5 marks)

b Link these five farming types with the following five descriptions:
 i) rearing cattle for milk,
 ii) a subsistence form of agriculture,
 iii) growing crops,
 iv) growing crops and rearing animals,
 v) hill farming.

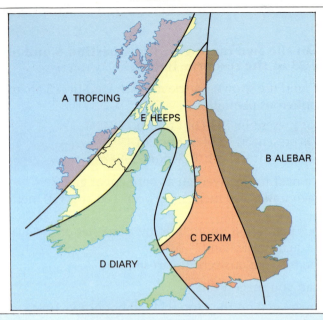

Figure 3h

10 Pages 22 and 23 of the resource book will help you to answer this question.

a Describe four physical features shown in the photograph, taken in the Lake District, and state how they have determined the type of farming found there. (4 marks)

b How does a farmer in the Lake District make use of both Zone A and Zone B? (4 marks)

c Explain why farming in the Lake District was once described as a 'traditional way of life' but is now described as 'marginal'. (2 marks)

d How can farmers in the Lake District increase their earnings? (2 marks)

LEAG,D 1988

Figure 3i

11 Refer to the Ordnance Survey map of Coventry on pages 76 and 77.

Lodge Farm is located at map reference 387818. Rewrite the following paragraph choosing the correct answer from each of the alternatives given in brackets.

a Lodge Farm is located (6/12 km) to the (NE/SW) of Coventry's city centre. It lies on land which is quite (steep/flat) and about (79/97) metres above sea-level. It is next to the (A45(T)/A46(T)) road and less than 1 km from motorway interchange number (2/6) on the (M5/M6). (7 marks)

b Lodge Farm is in a good position to grow fruit, flowers and vegetables
 i) Where will most of the produce be sold? (1 mark)
 ii) Name **two** other places, both within 2 kms of the farm, which might buy the fresh produce. (2 marks)

16

FARMING AND CHANGE

12 Use Figure 3j and refer to page 26 in the resource book.

Read the newspaper extract in Figure 3j carefully. It describes some of the effects of the greater use of fertiliser.

a Why has the use of nitrogen fertiliser increased? (1 mark)

b What is the EC's safe limit for nitrates in drinking water? (1 mark)

c What is said to be the effect of the pollution on:
  i) People?
  ii) Wildlife? (2 marks)

d Describe the distribution of the heavily polluted rivers. (3 marks)

e Give a reason for the distribution you have described in **d**. (2 marks)

f The left hand side of Figure 3k describes a healthy river ecosystem.
  i) What is meant by an ecosystem? (Refer to page 28 in the resource book). (2 marks)
  ii) Study the newspaper extract again. Use the blank boxes below to describe and explain the changes that take place in a polluted river. (6 marks)

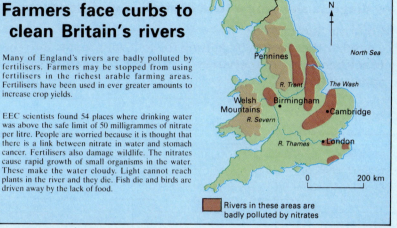

Figure 3j

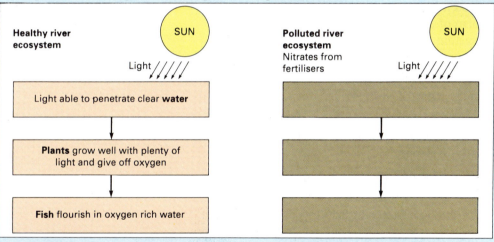

Figure 3k

MEG/WJUB,E 1988

13 Refer to page 27 in the resource book.

a i) Give **three** reasons why it is an advantage to some farmers to clear hedgerows? (3 marks)

  ii) Give **three** ways by which this removal can harm the environment. (3 marks)

b i) What do you understand by the term 'wetland'? (1 mark)
  ii) Why is it important to conserve our wetlands? (2 marks)
  iii) Why do farmers wish to reclaim 'wetlands' such as the Norfolk Broads? (1 mark)
  iv) What environmental problems are caused by the drainage of wetlands? (3 marks)
  v) What is meant by the term 'Environmentally Sensitive Areas' (ESAs)? (1 mark)
  vi) Give **two** advantages, one economic and one environmental, which should result from the creation of ESAs. (2 marks)

FOUR — FORESTRY AND LANDSCAPE

1 Refer to page 28 in the resource book. Study Figure 4a which is a flow diagram showing a food chain in a woodland ecosystem.

a i) Copy the flow diagram.
ii) Complete the diagram by putting the following words into the correct boxes:
   blackberries   carnivores   grouse   herbivores   sparrowhawk   (5 marks)

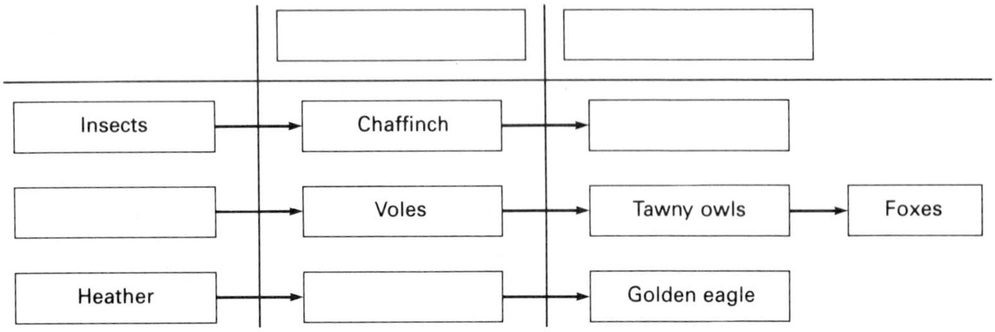

Figure 4a

```
        ┌──────────┐   ┌──────────┐
        │          │   │          │
────────┼──────────┼───┼──────────┼──────────────
 ┌──────┐    ┌──────────┐   ┌──────────┐
 │Insects│──▶│ Chaffinch │──▶│          │
 └──────┘    └──────────┘   └──────────┘
 ┌──────┐    ┌──────────┐   ┌──────────┐   ┌──────┐
 │      │──▶│   Voles   │──▶│Tawny owls│──▶│Foxes │
 └──────┘    └──────────┘   └──────────┘   └──────┘
 ┌──────┐    ┌──────────┐   ┌──────────┐
 │Heather│──▶│          │──▶│Golden eagle│
 └──────┘    └──────────┘   └──────────┘
```

b What do you understand by the terms:
 i) ecosystem,
 ii) food chain?   (2 marks)

c Using information given in Figure 4.1 in the resource book
 i) Name **three** inputs into the system.
 ii) Name **one** process and **one** form of storage within the system.
 iii) Name **two** outputs from the system.
 iv) Give **two** examples of recycling within the system.   (9 marks)

d i) How can people affect the inputs into this sytem?   (2 marks)
 ii) How can people alter the outputs from the system?   (2 marks)

2 Study the graph in Figure 4b below which shows the percentage of land use given over to forests in Britain.

a i) What percentage of the European Community (EC) is covered by forest?
 ii) What percentage of Great Britain is covered by forest?   (2 marks)

b i) By how many percent does Scotland exceed Great Britain's average in land covered by forest?
 ii) Which country has less than the average amount of forest cover in Great Britain?   (2 marks)

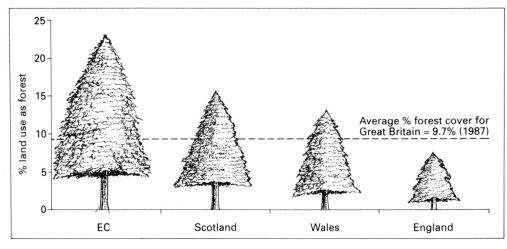

Figure 4b

3 Refer to page 29 in the resource book.

Study Figure 4c which shows how tree types alter with the height of the land.

a i) Which type of land use is found above the tree line?
   ii) Name the type of tree growing at the highest point of the diagram. (2 marks)

b Four types of coniferous tree are named in Figure 4c.
   i) Name the only one which is native to the British Isles.
   ii) Name the type of coniferous tree which originally came from:
   - Asia,
   - the mainland of Europe. (3 marks)

c i) What is the tree line? (1 mark)
   ii) Give **three** reasons why trees do not grow on the hill-tops. (3 marks)

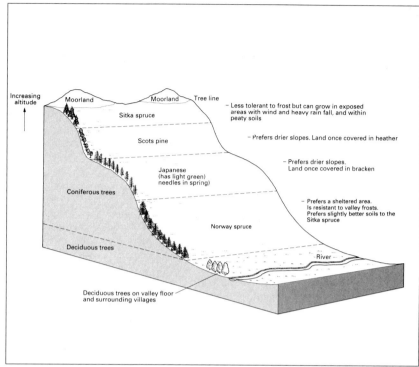

Figure 4c

d The most common tree in Britain is the spruce.
   i) In which type of soil do Sitka spruce grow the best?
   ii) Which type of spruce prefers a sheltered, slightly warmer climate?
   iii) Try to find out why frosts occur in valley bottoms. (3 marks)

e Which **two** types of tree prefer drier soils?

f Why is the Japanese larch considered to be attractive? (1 mark)

g Deciduous trees are found growing on the valley floor.
   i) Give **four** physical reasons why they grow here.
   ii) Give **one** environmental advantage of growing deciduous trees.
   iii) Give **two** economic advantages of growing coniferous trees. (7 marks)

4 Use the information given on page 30 of the resource book.

It is proposed to plant (afforest) a new area of woodland within a National Park. Before planning permission is given a public enquiry has to be held. If you had to speak at the meeting:
   i) Give reasons why you would be **either** in favour **or** against the scheme. (4 marks)
   ii) What would be the main arguments of your opponents? (4 marks)

5 Refer to pages 32 and 33 in the resource book.

a What attempts are being made to improve Britain's forests:
   i) visually,
   ii) for wild life,
   iii) for tourists? (3 marks)

b i) What problems might tourists create for forestry workers?
   ii) How might these problems be overcome? (4 marks)

c The summer of 1989 was very hot and dry. What problem did this create for the forestry worker? (1 mark)

FIVE WATER

1 Use page 34 of the resource book to answer this question.

a Of the ten statements given below, six are correct. Write out the correct ones.
(3 marks)

- There is always the same amount of water in and around the world.
- Most of the world's surface is covered in land.
- Only 30% of the world's surface is land, the rest is covered in water.
- Most water in the world is fresh.
- Fresh water is found in lakes and small seas.
- 96% of the world's water is in the seas and oceans.
- Most fresh water is in streams, rivers, lakes, ice or stored underground.
- The water cycle is about the flow of water in rivers.
- The water cycle is the name given to the natural process by which water is moved around the earth as water in rivers, lakes and oceans, as water vapour in the air, and as ice.
- Another name for the water cycle is the hydrological cycle.

b Give **six** uses for water. (3 marks)

2 a i) Make a copy of the graph outline shown in Figure 5b.
ii) Plot the water supply information given in Figure 5a as a line graph.
(The first three points have been plotted for you). (5 marks)
iii) Add labels and a suitable title. (2 marks)

b Which of the following statements best describes the changes in water supply shown by the graph?
- No real change.
- Rapid at first but slower increase later.
- Slow at first but rapid increase later.
- Overall increase but uneven with both ups and downs.
- Steady growth over many years. (1 mark)

c i) Continue your graph with a dotted line up to the year 2000. (1 mark)
ii) How much more water per day will be needed in the year 2000 than in 1987? (1 mark)
iii) Why is it so important for water authorities to know the present and future needs of water supply in Britain? (4 marks)

Figure 5b

Figure 5a

Average daily quantity of water supplied in England and Wales 1975 — 1987

Year	Million litres per day
1975	15 100
1976	14 500
1977	14 800
1978	15 400
1979	16 000
1980	15 900
1981	15 800
1982	16 300
1983	16 400
1984	16 600
1985	16 600
1986	16 900
1987	16 900

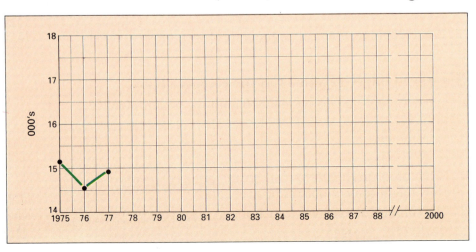

3 Page 34 of the resource book will give you help with this question.

a Make a copy of Figure 5c and complete it by writing in each of the following water cycle terms against the correct description.

**surface run-off   groundwater run-off   precipitation
condensation   evaporation**

Figure 5c

Water cycle term	Description
	All forms of moisture falling from clouds. Includes rain, drizzle, snow, sleet and hail.
	The flow of water over the land.
	The flow of water through soil and rocks below the surface.
	The process by which liquid water becomes water vapour.
	The change of water from its invisible water vapour state to a visible liquid such as cloud or fog.

b Study Figure 5d below which shows part of the hydrological (water) cycle.

i) Draw the diagram and complete it by putting the correct answer in each box. Choose your answers from the following list.

**condensation   evaporation   precipitation   surface run-off
transpiration**

Figure 5d

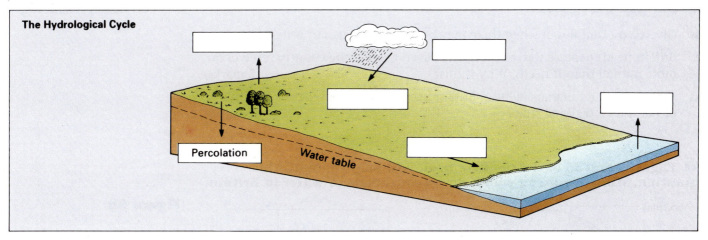

ii) What is meant by:
- percolation,   ■ water table?   (2 marks)

4 Refer to page 34 of the resource book

Study Figure 5e below which shows part of the hydrological cycle.
Copy and complete the diagram by putting the correct answers in each numbered box.
Choose your answers from the following list:

lakes and rivers   groundwater   land   sea

Figure 5e

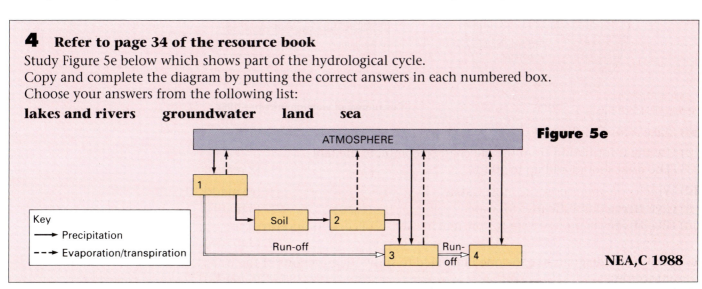

NEA,C 1988

WATER

5 Use pages 34 and 35 in the resource book to help answer this question.

Figure 5f is a flow diagram showing the problems of water supply.

a Copy the diagram and complete it by putting the following statements in the correct boxes.
- Cause problems
- Seasonal variations
- Supply located far from demand
- Require national water management plan. (4 marks)

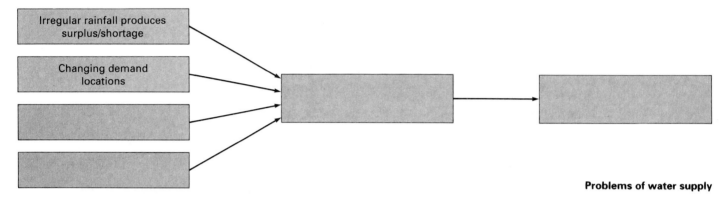

Figure 5f

Problems of water supply

b Give **two** examples of when there may be water shortages in Britain. (2 marks)

c Britain needs to store water in reservoirs even though the country receives far more rainfall than it needs. Why is this? (2 marks)

d Why does water management in Britain need to be organised on a national rather than a regional scale? (2 marks)

6 Pages 34 and 35 of the resource book will help you with this question. Study Figure 5g which shows consumers of water in Britain.

Figure 5g

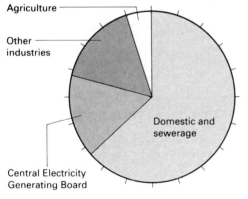

Use	%
Domestic and sewerage	
C E G B	
Other industries	
Agriculture	

Consumers of water in Britain — 1988

a i) Make a copy of the table.

ii) Use the information from the pie chart to complete the table. (The total should add up to 100%) (2 marks)

b i) Which consumer uses the most water? (1 mark)

ii) Give **three** domestic uses for water. (3 marks)

iii) Give **three** examples to show how much water is needed for industrial use. (3 marks)

c Draw a star diagram like the one illustrated to show the functions of the water authorities. (6 marks)

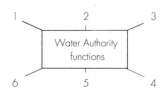

7 Refer to page 35 in the resource book.
People interrupt and alter the water cycle to satisfy some of their needs. One of these needs is a water supply.

Study Figure 5h, it shows where some of our cities get their water from.

a Where does Birmingham get its water from? (1 mark)

b How far does Birmingham's water have to travel? (1 mark)

c Name **two** Water Authorities that transfer water to other authorities. (2 marks)

d Give **two** reasons why some areas have a surplus of water while other areas have too little.
Reason 1
Reason 2 (2 marks)

MEG,E 1988

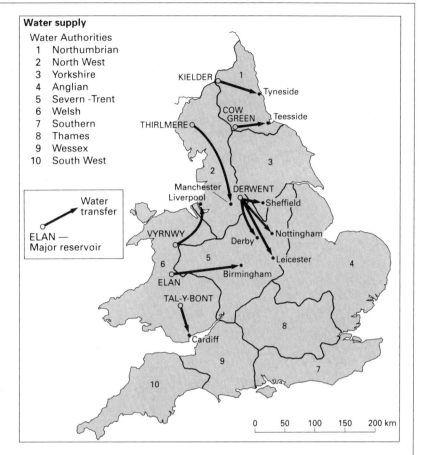

Figure 5h

---

8 Pages 35 to 37 of the resource book will help you with this question.
Study Figure 5i below which gives information about two possible reservoir sites in rural areas.

Figure 5i

	Site X	Site Y
Location	Central Wales	Eastern England
Relief	High ground	Low ground
Dam height needed	50 metres	15 metres
Dam length needed	150 metres	400 metres
Land to be flooded	1 square kilometre	6 square kilometres
Present land use	Rough grazing for sheep	Mixed arable and beef land
Soil quality	Poor grade	High grade
Houses to be submerged	Three	Thirty
Roads to be submerged	Two	Twelve

a State which site you recommend as being the best site for a major reservoir. (1 mark)

b Give **three** advantages of your chosen site. (3 marks)

c The people living in the area of the proposed reservoir will probably object to your chosen site.
  i) Give **three** possible objections they might have.
  ii) Suggest **two** possible benefits to the area, other than water supply, which you feel might encourage them to be more willing to accept the scheme. (5 marks)

LEAG,B 1988

WATER

9 Pages 36 and 37 of the resource book will help you to answer this question.

a Figure 5j below is a sketch of Kielder Water based on the aerial photograph, Figure 5.6 in the resource book.
Use the photograph and map (Figure 5.9 on page 37 of the resource book) to help answer the following questions.

 i) Make an accurate copy of the sketch. (1 mark)

 ii) Make the sketch clearer by shading lightly in pencil to make the water blue, the forest dark green and the moorland and farmland light green.
Add those colours to the key. (3 marks)

Kielder Water
Kielder forest
Moorland and farmland

A =
B =
C =
D =
E =
F =

Sketch of Kielder Water

Distance between the two Information centres _____

Figure 5j

 iii) Complete the key using the following information;

- Kielder Castle information centre
- Tower Knowe information centre
- Kielder Dam
- Bakethin Dam
- New road — C200
- Falstone village. (3 marks)

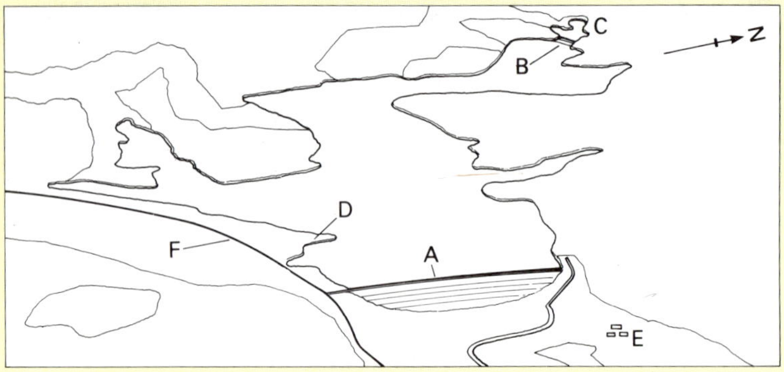

 iv) Which of the following is the straight line distance between the two information centres? Write your answer in the key.
(Use the sketch and resource book map).
4 km   6 km   7.5 km   9.5 km   12 km (1 mark)

b Describe the main features of the Kielder project. (2 marks)

c Why was Kielder needed? (2 marks)

d Give reasons for Kielder being chosen as a reservoir site by joining up the following sentence beginnings with the correct endings. (3 marks)

Beginnings
- Limited effect on local area because of —
- Narrow part of valley —
- Sound underlying rock —
- Large water catchment area —
- Dam making materials available nearby —
- Regular and heavy rainfall in the area —

Endings
- provides good base to build dam.
- keeps reservoir filled up.
- poor farming land and few people.
- make dam construction easier.
- collects maximum volume of water.
- allows for shorter, cheaper dam.

e The Kielder project is a multi-purpose scheme that provides:
- Water for domestic and industrial use.
- Water control for the Tyne valley.
- Electricity for the National Grid.
- Recreational facilities.

 i) Draw a star diagram to show the four main uses of the Kielder project. (1 mark)

 ii) What is the meaning of the term 'Multi-purpose scheme'? (1 mark)

 iii) List **eight** amenities that tourists may use in the Kielder area. (4 marks)

10 Refer to pages 35, 36 and 37 in the resource book.

For Kielder or any river you have studied which has been changed for economic purposes:

a i) Name the river or scheme.
ii) State where the river or scheme is located. (1 mark)
iii) Describe the purpose of the scheme. (2 marks)

b i) State **three** ways in which the scheme may benefit people in the local area. (3 marks)

ii) State **three** problems that the scheme may cause for people in the local area. (3 marks)

iii) Describe the changes to the natural environment of the local area caused by the scheme. (2 marks)

c How successful do you consider the scheme has been? Give reasons for your answer. (5 marks)

11 Refer to pages 34 to 37 in the resource book.

Study Figures 5k and 5l which show the changes brought about by the creation of Ladybower reservoir in the Peak District National Park.

a i) Between which two large cities is Ladybower reservoir located? (1 mark)
ii) How far is it from the old dam to the new dam? (1 mark)
iii) Which **two** rivers feed Ladybower reservoir. (1 mark)
iv) Name the **two** villages flooded by the reservoir. (1 mark)

b Imagine that you lived in one of the villages that was flooded by the new reservoir
Write a letter to a friend explaining why you had to move and what your feelings were when you first heard of the reservoir plans
Your letter should be about a page in length. (8 marks)

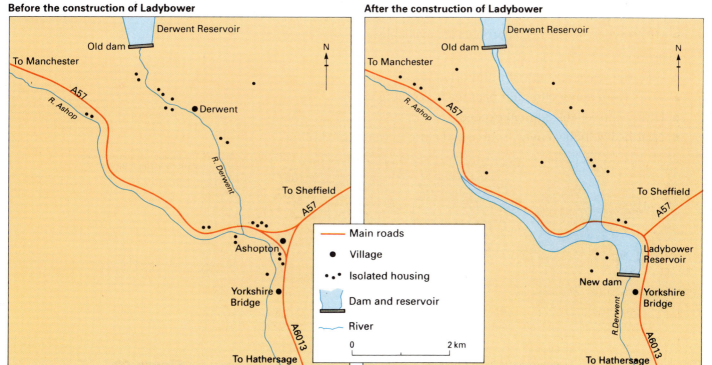

Figure 5k
Before the construction of Ladybower

Figure 5l
After the construction of Ladybower

SIX ENERGY — SUPPLY AND DEMAND

1 Refer to pages 38-47 in the resource book.
Study Figure 6a which gives information about various energy resources.
Use the information to complete the table below. (10 marks)

Energy source	Advantages	Disadvantages

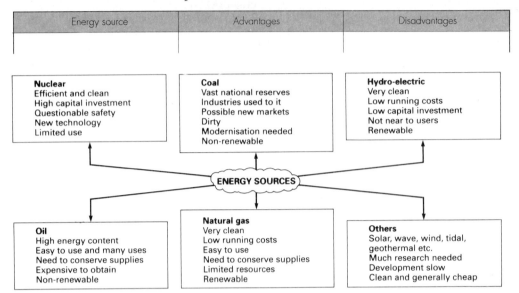

Figure 6a

2 Refer to page 38 in the resource book.
Figure 6b below shows the location of some power stations in Great Britain. Copy and complete the diagram by adding the following information in the correct places.

Type: ■ nuclear   ■ hydro-electric   ■ oil   ■ coal

Location:
- Mainly in upland areas of NW Scotland and N Wales
- Mainly on the coast
- On coalfields, near rivers or on the coast
- On the coast where deep harbours are available

Reason:
- Near to coastal refineries for imported raw material
- Away from major cities but near sea for cooling water
- Heavy and reliable rainfall needed
- Near heavy, bulky energy source and close to water for cooling

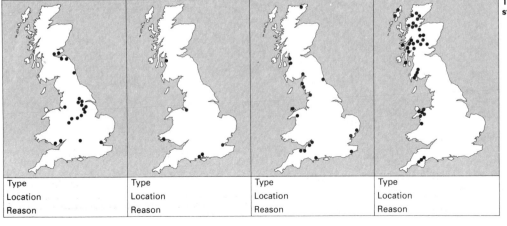

The location of some power stations in Great Britain

Figure 6b

ENERGY SUPPLY AND DEMAND

3 Refer to pages 38 and 39 in the resource book.
Study Figure 6c which is a divided bar graph showing the source of Britain's energy supply between 1950 and 1980.

Figure 6c

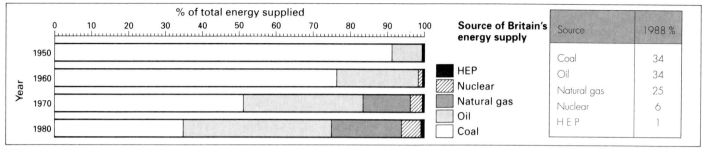

a Construct a divided bar graph to show the source of Britain's energy supply in 1988. (5 marks)

b i) Which source supplied most of Britain's energy in 1950? (1 mark)
   ii) Which energy source has declined most in importance between 1950 and 1988? (1 mark)
   iii) Which energy sources have increased in importance between 1950 and 1988? (3 marks).

c Give **three** reasons why an energy resource may decline in importance. (3 marks)

d Britain's energy policy is:

   'To secure energy needs at the lowest possible cost in resources and money through conservation and the efficient use of the most appropriate fuels.'

   Because the price and availability of resources may vary considerably it is important that an energy policy can use several different types of energy source.

   i) What is meant by conservation? (1 mark)
   ii) What is meant by efficient? (1 mark)
   iii) In which of the following years did Britain have the best energy policy?
   1950, 1960, 1970, 1980, 1987.
   Give reasons for your answer. (3 marks)

Figure 6d

4 Refer to pages 38 and 39 in the resource book.
Study Figure 6d which shows some estimates as to how long the various sources of energy may last if used at current levels.

a Which of the energy sources shown is not a fossil fuel? (1 mark)

b Apart from the production of electricity, give three uses for oil. (3 marks)

c In which year is it expected that there will be a major shortage of oil? (1 mark)

d Give **two** reasons that make it very difficult to estimate how long a resource may last. (2 marks)

e Alternative energy sources are not shown in Figure 6d:
   i) What is the meaning of the term 'alternative energy'? (1 mark)
   ii) Give one example of an alternative energy source. (1 mark)
   iii) Why do conservation groups usually support the development of alternative energy supplies? (2 marks)

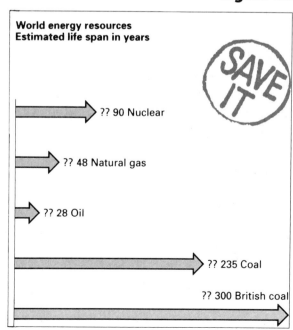

ENERGY SUPPLY AND DEMAND

5 Refer to pages 38, 40 and 41 in the resource book.

Of the following ten statements, six are correct. Write out the correct ones.

(3 marks)

- Britain changed to other energy sources in 1955 because oil was too costly.
- Britain increased its use of oil because it was a clean, efficient energy source.
- Britain increased its use of oil because it was cheap to buy from the Middle East.
- More oil is needed in Britain to supply the expanding transport and road system.
- North Sea gas was discovered in 1965 off the coast of East Anglia.
- North Sea oil was discovered in 1952.
- Most gas fields are in the southern part of the North Sea.
- North Sea gas was discovered in 1970.
- Oil fields are scattered evenly all over the North Sea.
- Most oil fields are in the northern part of the North Sea.

6 Refer to pages 40 and 41 in the resource book.

Copy and complete the crossword in Figure 6e.
Choose your answers from the following list.

(5 marks)

Ninian
Ekofisk
Sullom Voe
Argyll
Nigg
Claymore
Cruden Bay
Piper
Flotta
Murchison
Forties
Teesside
Brent
Montrose
St Fergus

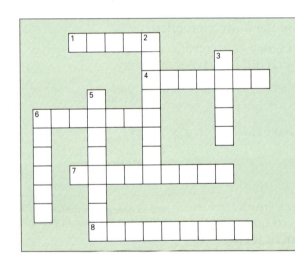

Figure 6e

Across
1 A main northern oil field.
4 A southern oil field at the end of a main pipeline.
6 A main oil field 175 km NE of Aberdeen.
7 A mainland oil terminal in Scotland.
8 A major northern oil terminal.

Down
2 A major oil terminal 350 km SW of Ekofisk.
3 An oil field 150 km east of Cruden Bay.
5 The mainland end of a gas pipeline.
6 An island oil terminal.

7 Refer to page 40 in the resource book.

To show the problems of North Sea oil and gas, copy and complete Figure 6f by adding a short sentence of explanation to each box. (Two have already been completed to help you.) (10 marks)

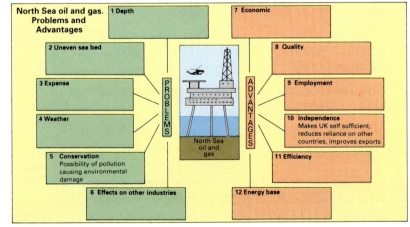

Figure 6f

ENERGY SUPPLY AND DEMAND

8 Refer to pages 42 and 43 in the resource book.
There have been many changes in the main uses of coal in the UK during the last 40 years.
Study Figure 6g which shows some of these changes.

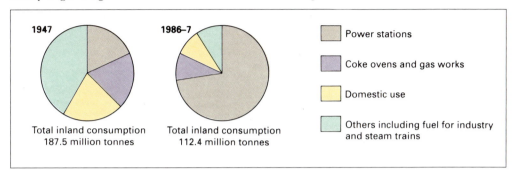

Figure 6g

a i) What was the main use of coal in: (1) 1947 and (2) 1987? (2 marks)
  ii) What was the % of coal used in power stations in: (1) 1947 and (2) 1987?
  (2 marks)

b i) What would be the main domestic use for coal in 1947? (1 mark)
  ii) What new energy source has caused a decline in the number of gas works needed? (1 mark)

c i) Describe the changes in coal use during the period 1947 to 1987. (2 marks)
  ii) Suggest reasons for these changes. (2 marks)

9 Refer to pages 42 and 43 in the resource book.
Study Figure 6h which shows information about the British coal industry between 1947 and 1987.

a What does the graph tell you about:
  i) The total output of coal since 1947? (1 mark)
  ii) The amount of coal produced per miner since 1947? (1 mark)
  iii) How the number of coal mines has changed since 1947? (1 mark)

b Although the total output of coal has shown a decrease since 1947, each mine now produces more coal than in 1947. Give **two** reasons which account for this change. (2 marks)

c Give **three** reasons to account for the fact that we need so much less coal today than we did in 1947. (3 marks)

10 An important issue in Britain's future energy plan is whether coal will still be a major source of energy in the 1990s.

a Describe the arguments presented by the two sides in favour of and against the use of coal as a major source of energy in the 1990s.

b What is your opinion about the issue?

c Justify your views. (10 marks)

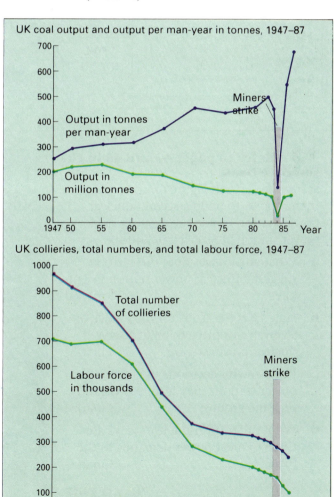

Figure 6h

ENERGY SUPPLY AND DEMAND

11 Refer to pages 44 and 45 in the resource book.
The following is a list of arguments both for and against nuclear energy.
Copy and complete Figure 6i by writing the statements in the correct boxes.

- Small amounts of raw materials used.
- Use will cause closure of some coal mines.
- Worries over safety.
- Nuclear power can not provide all power needs.
- Fossil fuels are best used for other things.
- Will replace dirty coal.
- Demand for electricity is decreasing.
- Renewable resources should be used for electricity production.

b Imagine that plans have been proposed to locate a nuclear power station within 50 km of where you live. As a home owner and one who is against nuclear energy, write a letter to your MP arguing against the proposal. Your letter should be about a page in length. (10 marks)

c Imagine that you work for the Government in the Department of Energy. Draw a poster to describe to the public the benefits of nuclear energy. The poster should be attractive and colourful, have impact and clearly state the facts. (10 marks)

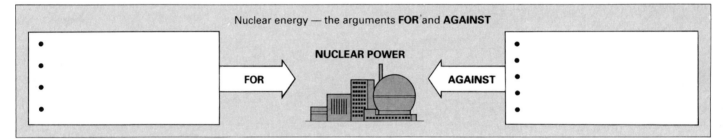

Figure 6i

12 Refer to pages 44 and 45 in the resource book.
Study the cartoon Figure 6j, concerning the proposal to build a second nuclear power station beside the existing nuclear power station at Sizewell in Suffolk.

a What advantages does the cartoon suggest a nuclear power station might have? (2 marks)

b State **three** reasons for the choice of Sizewell as a place to build a second nuclear power station. (3 marks)

c Explain why decisions to build nuclear power stations may lead to protests by pressure groups. (3 marks)

d What other (non-nuclear) ways are there to meet power demands in the future? (3 marks)

NEA, D 1987

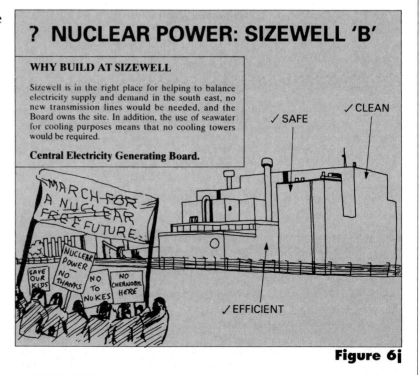

Figure 6j

ENERGY SUPPLY AND DEMAND

13 Refer to pages 44 to 47 in the resource book.

a i) What is the meaning of the term 'non-renewable (finite) energy resource'?
(1 mark)
ii) What is the meaning of the term 'renewable (infinite) energy resource'?
(1 mark)

Sources of Energy	
Renewable	Non-renewable

Figure 6k

b Use the wordsearch to find **ten** energy sources. The words read across, downwards and diagonally. Copy the table Figure 6k and list the energy sources in the correct columns.

c For each of the four 'downwords' in the wordsearch:
 i) Name the type of energy source.
 ii) Briefly describe how energy is produced using this source. (1 mark)
 iii) State the advantages of this type of energy source. (2 marks)
 iv) State the disadvantages of this type of energy source. (2 marks)

d i) Give **five** arguments against relying on renewable resources as sources of energy in Britain. (5 marks)
ii) What are the advantages of using renewable resources as sources of energy? (2 marks)

```
R S M T T O T V S L T O A I
L H P K R B I O G A S X E W
E T Y I B Z D L P Q M N W C
L V I D P L A V M S R W I R
N A T U R A L G A S Z X N M
J I L H K O O P Q W U O D K
W G E O T H E R M A L R I C
E N O V W B G L J V P L O L
K R U X Y D U U E E W M E C
```

Figure 6l

14 Refer to pages 44 and 45 in the resource book.
Hydro-electric power (HEP) is a clean and cheap method of energy production which is particularly attractive because it uses a renewable resource.

a Copy and complete Figure 6m below by adding the following labels:
- Heavy, reliable rainfall
- Generator producing electricity
- Power lines to National grid
- Water returned at off-peak times
- Reservoir for water storage and supply
- Water flowing through pipes or tunnels
- Water outlet to lake
- Dam
(4 marks)

b Describe how hydro-electric power is produced. (2 marks)
c What are the advantages of HEP as a source of energy? (2 marks)
d Draw a star diagram to show the needs of a hydro-electric power station.
(3 marks)

Figure 6m

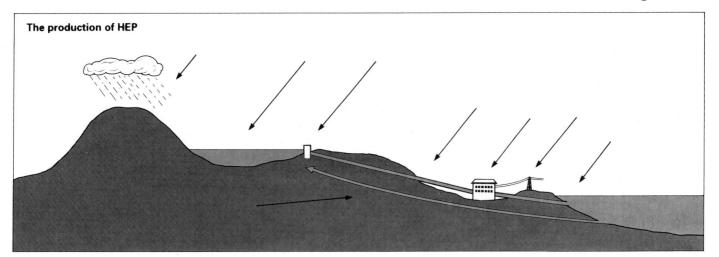

The production of HEP

SEVEN INDUSTRY AND CHANGE

1 Page 48 in the resource book will help you with this question.
Study Figure 7a which shows some of the physical and human factors which influence the location of industry.

a i) Make a copy of the diagram.
  ii) Add a further four labels to show other factors that are important in locating industries. (4 marks)

b Copy the table below and list the physical and human factors from your diagram in the correct columns. (8 marks)

c Choose **two** physical factors and **two** human factors and explain how they affect where industry should be located. (8 marks)

d i) What was the main location factor for older long established nineteenth century industries? (1 mark)
  ii) What three location factors are important for late twentieth century modern industries? (3 marks)

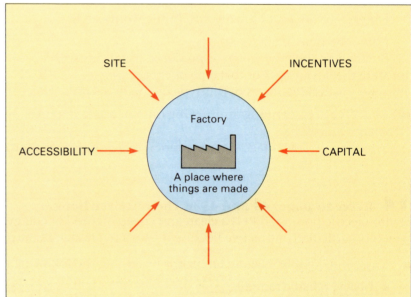

Figure 7a

2 Study Figure 7b. Refer also to pages 48 of the resource book.
Raw materials, markets and skilled labour have varying degrees of influence on the location of different industries. For example, diagram 1 shows that all three are equally important in deciding the location of a factory.

Figure 7b

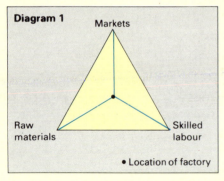 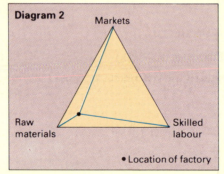 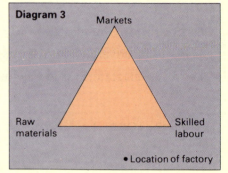

a i) Which of the three factors had the greatest influence on factory location in diagram 2? (1 mark)
  ii) What kind of industry is most likely to be located in the factory on diagram 2? Explain your answer. (3 marks)

b i) Copy diagram 3 and on it place a dot in what you consider to be the position which best corresponds to the needs of an electronics factory which has a research department attached to it. (1 mark)
  ii) Give **two** reasons why you chose that position for the location of a factory. (2 marks)

NEA,B 1988

INDUSTRY AND CHANGE

3 **Refer to page 49 in the resource book.**

Study Figure 7c which shows changes in unemployment in the UK from 1979 to 1990.

a How many people were unemployed in 1979? (1 mark)

b i) In which year were most people unemployed? (1 mark)

ii) How many were unemployed in that year? (1 mark)

c How many were unemployed in 1990? (1 mark)

d Describe the changes in unemployment shown by the graph. (3 marks)

e Give **three** reasons for industrial decline and increased unemployment. (3 marks)

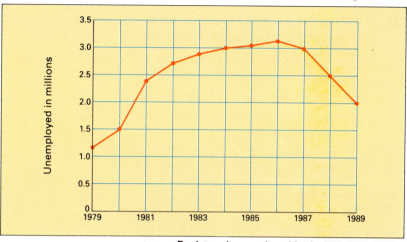

Figure 7c

Registered unemployed in the UK, 1979–1989

4 **Refer to page 49 in the resource book.**

Although unemployment is found in all regions in Britain, some areas do show job gains over a period of time.
Study Figure 7d.

a Name **three** areas which have over 9% of people unemployed (3 marks)

b Which **two** regions have the highest number of job losses? (2 marks)

c Which area has less than 5% of people unemployed and the most job gains? (1 mark)

d Which of the following statements best describe the pattern of unemployment and job losses in Britain? (2 marks)

- The percentage of people unemployed is greatest in the south.
- Only the east of Britain has a high percentage of people unemployed.
- The north and west of Britain has the highest percentage of people unemployed and the most job losses.
- The South East and East Anglia are the regions with the lowest percentage of people unemployed and the most job gains.

Figure 7d

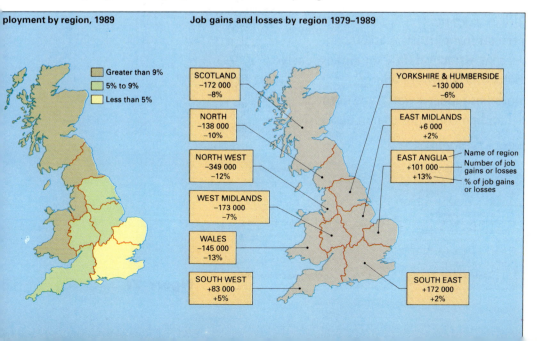

INDUSTRY AND CHANGE

5 Refer to pages 49 to 52 in the resource book. Study Figure 7e.

a What has been a major cause of job loss in the north and west of Britain during the last 20 years? (1 mark)

b What has been a major cause of job loss in Northern Ireland, Scotland and the Northern region during the last 20 years? (1 mark)

c Which areas have suffered job losses in the last 20 years due to the introduction of machinery and modern methods in farming? (2 marks)

d Select **one** example of a primary industry (where food or raw materials are produced) which has suffered job losses in the last 20 years.
 i) Name your example.
 ii) State in which region or regions it has caused job losses. (1 mark)
 iii) Suggest **two** reasons for these job losses. (2 marks)

Figure 7e

6 Refer to pages 49 and 50 in the resource book.
Figure 7f below shows some causes of colliery closure and job losses in the South Wales coalmining industry.

a Make a large copy of Figure 7f.

b Describe each cause by adding the following information to the correct boxes. (4 marks)

- Easily obtained coal used up. Difficult and expensive to mine remaining seams.
- Not sufficient money invested by government to improve efficiency.
- Pay increases caused coal prices to go up.
- South Wales coalfield located far from British markets.
- Outdated machinery makes coal extraction difficult and expensive.
- Government actively supports other forms of energy.
- Automation in modern mines has reduced workforce needed.
- Increased coal prices caused foreign countries to purchase elsewhere.

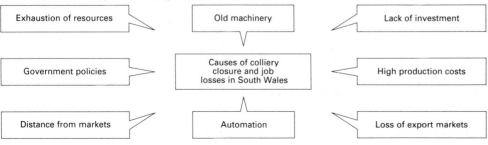

Figure 7f

INDUSTRY AND CHANGE

7 **Refer to page 51 in the resource book.**
Figure 7g shows how employment has changed in Corby since 1934.

a Make a copy of Figure 7g.

b Complete the graph using the following figures.
Total workforce: 1981 — 15 000,   1986 — 19 500.
Steelworkers: 1981 — 4 500,   1986 — 2 000.   (4 marks)

c Show the changes in economic activity in Corby by printing the following information in the correct boxes.   (4 marks)

- 13 000 workers and over half of workforce employed in steel.
- Closure of steel works and massive job losses.
- Steel and steel tube industry started.
- New economic growth with balanced industrial base.

d i) Why was Corby chosen as a site for a steel works?   (1 mark)
   ii) Why are many families in Corby of Scottish origin?   (1 mark)
   iii) What is meant by the term 'a one industry town'?   (1 mark)
   iv) Why did the steelworks close?   (1 mark)
   v) How did the tube works remain open after Corby steelworks closed? (1 mark)
   vi) Give **four** reasons for recent industrial growth in Corby. (4 marks)

e Explain why it is better for a town to have a variety of industries rather than rely on a single one as happened with British Steel in Corby.   (2 marks)

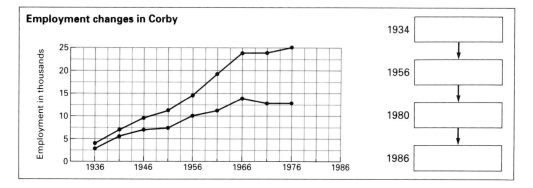

Figure 7g

8 **Refer to pages 49 and 51 in the resource book.**
Read the recent headline and newspaper extract in Figure 7h.

Figure 7h

> **End of a great shipbuilding industry**
>
> With the final closure of the Austin and Pickersgill shipyard in Sunderland fears are growing as to whether shipbuilding has any future in this country. Particularly worrying is the plight of shipyard workers who face bleak times with little early prospect of alternative employment.

a Use the following headings to help explain the decline in British shipbuilding

   i) fall in demand,
   ii) production costs,
   iii) competition,
   iv) rationalisation.   (4 marks)

b Why might it be particularly difficult for shipbuilding workers to gain alternative employment? (Clue: worker skills, decline of similar industries.)
                                                                (2 marks)

c Help from the government in the form of subsidies can sometimes save struggling industries from closure.

Give **one** advantage and **one** disadvantage of this type of help.   (2 marks)

INDUSTRY AND CHANGE

9 Refer also to pages 42, 43, 56, 57 and 122 in the resource book.

a Study the photograph (Figure 7i) which shows an industrial area in South Wales.
  i) Describe **three** of the main features of the industrial estate shown in the photograph. (3 marks)
  ii) For **each** of the **three** features that you have described, suggest a reason for their importance. (3 marks)
  iii) Why has the government encouraged the building of industrial estates? (2 marks)
  iv) Name **one** resource shown in the area of the photograph. (1 mark)
  v) Is the resource you have named renewable or non-renewable? (1 mark)

b Such industrial estates attract 'footloose' industries.
  i) What is a footloose industry? (1 mark)
  ii) Name **two** ways that a government, local authority or development agency can encourage a footloose industry to set up in a particular location. (2 marks)

Figure 7i

SEG,A 1988

10 Refer to pages 56 and 57 in the resource book.
The outskirts of cities are now popular locations for both new industries and for industries that wish to move away from their original location in the old inner city.

a i) Make a large copy of Figure 7j.
  ii) Write a sentence in each space to show the reasons for industrial change. (8 marks)

b For an industrial estate, trading estate, business park or science park that you have studied which is located on the outskirts of a city:
  i) Name the estate and nearest town. (1 mark)
  ii) Draw a sketch map to show its location. (2 marks)
  iii) Describe the types of firm found there. (2 marks)
  iv) Suggest **three** reasons why these firms have set up business there. (3 marks)

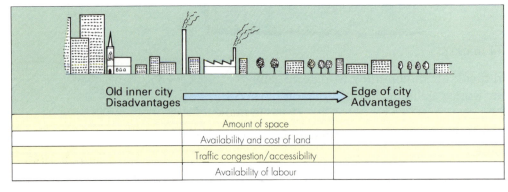

Figure 7j

INDUSTRY AND CHANGE

11 Refer to pages 54 to 56 in the resource book.
Study Figure 7k, which shows a part of the British Isles which is attracting a wide range of employment.

a Which motorway links London with Newport? (1 mark)

b What is the distance from London to Newport? (1 mark)

c From the map, give one example of a secondary industry and one example of a tertiary industry. (2 marks)

d How many high technology firms are shown on the map? (1 mark)

e State **three** reasons from the map, which would explain why high technology firms and other modern industries, are found in this area. (3 marks)

f Why is an attractive countryside an important factor in the location of modern industry? (2 marks)

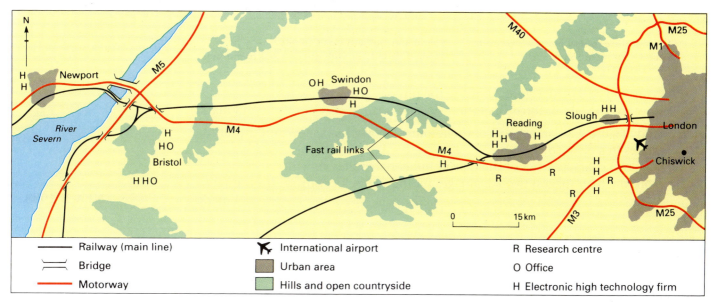

Figure 7k

12 Refer to pages 54 and 55 in the resource book.
Figure 7l shows the different locations which a firm making electronic components has occupied in the last eight years.
The map, in Figure 7k is of the same area.

Figure 7l

Date	Place	Area	Employees	Accomodation	Land value
1979	Chiswick, London	140 m²	13	Room above a garage	Very expensive
1982	Slough	325 m²	70	Took over existing building (1930s)	Expensive
1987	Swindon outskirts	65 000 m²	600+	Purpose built in a Business Park on the outskirts alongside M4	Less expensive

Use the table to explain why the firm decided to move:

a from Chiswick to Slough, (3 marks)

b from Slough to Swindon. (3 marks)

NEA, B 1988

INDUSTRY AND CHANGE

13 Refer to pages 56 and 57 in the resource book.

a Study Figure 7m which gives information about changes in manufacturing industry between the nineteenth century and the late twentieth century.

Figure 7m

	19th century industry	Late 20th century industry
Raw materials	Large quantities needed	Small quantities needed, often from other factories
Labour force	Large labour force, mainly male	Small labour force, mainly female
End products	Often bulky and difficult to move	Often small and easy to move
Transport		
Location		

Located close to raw materials or ports **Found near railways and canals**
Found near main roads **Located close to or with good access to markets**

i) Copy and complete Figure 7m using the phrases given below it.
ii) How has the labour force changed? (3 marks)

b Study Figure 7.26 on page 57 of the resource book which shows industrial estates in a New Town.
i) Give two characteristics of the type of industrial estates shown.
ii) From the map suggest two advantages for industries locating on these estates.
(4 marks)

NEA, B 1988

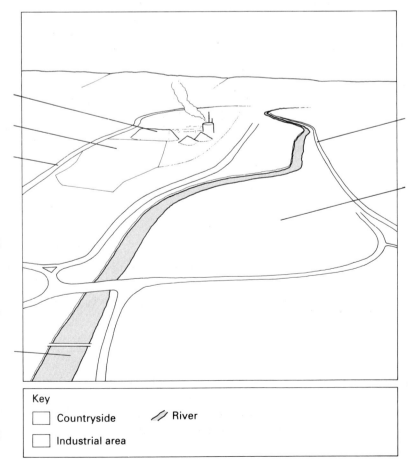

Figure 7n

14 Refer to pages 56 and 57 in the resource book.
Figure 7n is a sketch of an industrial area in South Wales based on the photograph in Figure 7i.

a Make an accurate copy of the sketch.
(1 mark)

b Add the following labels to the sketch.
**motorway coal stockpile
railway industrial estate
river pleasant countryside
flat ground available for development**
(7 marks)

c Make the sketch clearer by shading lightly in pencil — the countryside green, the river blue, and the industrial area brown. (1 mark)

d Complete the key and add a suitable title
(2 marks)

Key: Countryside, River, Industrial area

INDUSTRY AND CHANGE

15 Refer to page 52 in the resource book.

a What is meant by each of the following types of industry or economic activity:
 i) primary activity,
 ii) secondary activity,
 iii) tertiary activity,
 iv) quaternary activity? (4 marks)

Figure 7o

Grid reference	Name of industry or economic activity	Type of activity (primary, secondary or tertiary)
382804	Hospital	Tertiary
415784		
303818		
355744		
301759		

b Study the Ordnance Survey map of Coventry on pages 76 and 77.
 i) Copy Figure 7o above.
 ii) Name the industry or economic activity at each grid reference and state whether it is primary, secondary or tertiary.
  (The first one has been done to help you.) (8 marks)

16 Refer to page 52 in the resource book.

a Use the wordsearch to find 18 different types of jobs. The words read across and downwards.

b Sort the jobs into primary, secondary and tertiary. (18 marks)

17 Refer to page 52 in the resource book.
Figure 7p shows the occupations of the people in a town.

a Which of the following statements are correct?
- Most people are employed in tertiary occupations.
- Fewer people follow primary occupations than either of the other types.
- About a third of the people follow primary occupations.
- About a quarter of the people follow secondary occupations. (2 marks)

b Which of the following two statements is likely to be a correct description of the town?

Give reasons for your answer.
- The town is likely to be industrial with many old factories that now rely mainly on imported raw materials.
- The town is likely to have job opportunities in farming, forestry, making agricultural equipment and tourism. (3 marks)

Figure 7p

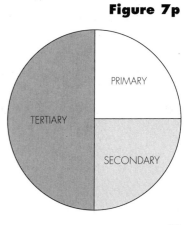

EIGHT RESIDENTIAL ENVIRONMENTS

1 Refer to pages 58 to 67 in the resource book

Make a copy of Figure 8a which gives a number of urban definitions and complete it by:

a Writing the following words or terms against the correct descriptions:
settlement   residential   urban sprawl   conurbation   (4 marks)

b Writing brief descriptions of the terms **urban area** and **rural area**. (2 marks)

Figure 8a

Word/Term	Description
	A place where people have settled down to live. e.g. a few houses, a village or a town.
Urban area	
Urban growth	The increase in the total number of people living in towns and cities.
Urbanisation	The increasing proportion of people living in towns and cities.
	The spreading of a city into the surrounding countryside.
	A very large urban area formed when towns or cities merge together.
	A place where people live. An area of housing.
Rural area	

2 Refer to page 58 in the resource book.

a i) Make a copy of the graph outline shown in Figure 8b.

ii) Plot the population information for London given in Figure 8c as a line graph. (The first three have been done to help you. Be careful plotting 1986.)
(8 marks)

iii) Add labels and a suitable title. (2 marks)

b Describe the changes in growth that have taken place in London between 1801 and 1986. (You should mention overall change and say when growth was slowest, when growth was most rapid and when a decrease in population occurred.) (3 marks)

c Does the graph show urban growth or urbanisation? Give a reason for your answer. (3 marks)

Figure 8b

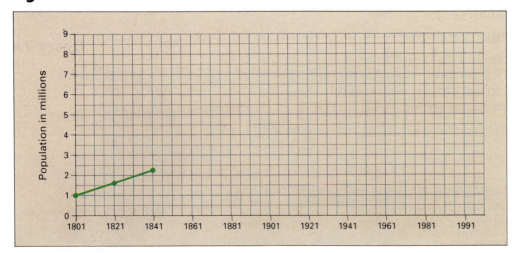

Figure 8c

Year	Population (millions)
1801	1.1
1821	1.6
1841	2.1
1861	3.1
1881	4.4
1901	6.2
1921	7.3
1941	8.4
1961	8.2
1981	6.7
1986	6.8

RESIDENTIAL ENVIRONMENTS

3 **Refer to page 58 in the resource book**
Study Figure 8d which shows where people lived in Britain between 1801 and 1981.

a Make a copy of Figure 8e and complete the table using information from Figure 8d. (4 marks)

b Of the five statements below, three are correct. Write out the correct ones. (3 marks)

- In the 1900s Britain's population has been mainly urban.
- Britain's population was mainly rural until 1951.
- In 1981 most of Britain's population lived in villages.
- Urbanisation has slowed down since 1901.
- In the early 1800s Britain's population was mainly rural.

c Do the pie charts in Figure 8d show **urban growth** or **urbanisation**? Give a reason for your answer. (3 marks)

d List **six** reasons why people move into cities. (3 marks)

e Imagine that you live in a city and have a friend who lives in a small village in the countryside and is about to leave school.
The friend is trying to decide whether to stay in the small village or move to the city.
Write a letter to the friend describing the advantages of living in a city.
(Your letter should be about a page in length.) (10 marks)

4 **Refer to pages 58 and 59 in the resource book.**
Figure 8f is a simplified model of land use in a typical British city.

a i) Make a large copy of Figure 8f.
ii) Describe and explain land use in a 'model' city by adding the following statements to the correct boxes. (4 marks)

- Mainly modern housing on edge of the city where space is available.
- Older housing area within walking distance of city centre and older factories.
- Offices and shops in city centre which is easiest place to get to.
- Open countryside with villages used by workers from the city.

b For a town or city that you know, give named examples for each of the four land use types given above. (4 marks)

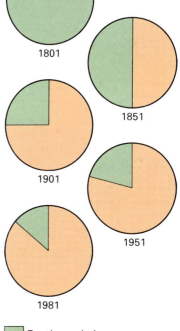

Changes in Britain's urban – rural population, 1801–1981

Figure 8d

Year	Rural	Urban
1801	75	25
1851		
1901		
1951		80
1981		

Figure 8e

Figure 8f

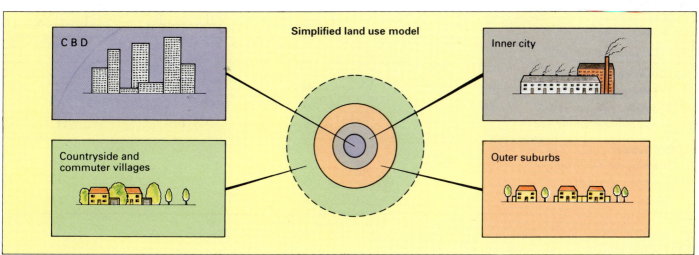

Residential areas	Some definitions
Design	The type of building, what it looks like
Detached	Single house with land around it.
Semi-detached	A house joined to another house on one side only.
Terraced	Houses built in a row with each house joined to the one next to it.
High-rise flats	Tall buildings containing many flats.
Multi-storey	Same as high rise.
Tenure	The way in which a house is occupied.
Owner - occupied	Housing owned by the people who live in it.
Rented-council	Rented housing built by and owned by the local authority.
Private-rented	Property owned privately and rented out to others.
Residents	People who live in a property or neighbourhood.
Household	A single person or group of people living in one property, e.g. a family.
Redevelopment	The demolition of a building or area and its replacement by new buildings.
Quality of environment	A measure of how pleasant a place is to live in.

Residential areas	Some definitions
Amenities	These are things or facilities that people need. They may be inside or outside a house, e.g. hot water, baths, parks, shops, transport.
Social class	This reflects a person's wealth, education, status and power. A person's occupation or socio-economic group is a good guide to this.
Professional/ managerial	Employers, managers and professional workers and other occupations with high salaries. Top qualifications are usually needed, e.g. dentist, lawyer.
Non-manual	Jobs where the main requirement is not physical effort, e.g. typist.
Skilled manual	Occupations that require special training, need mainly physical effort and are usually done by hand, e.g. carpenter, welder.
Semi-skilled	Jobs that require skills that are easily learned, e.g. bus driver, clerk.
Unskilled	Jobs that require no specific training, e.g. building labourer, roadsweeper.

Figure 8g

Figure 8h

Residential areas — census data	**Old inner city** e.g.	**Inner city redevelopment** e.g. Hyde Park, Sheffield	**Suburbia** e.g.	**Outer city council estate** e.g. Kenton, Newcastle
Tenure Council rented Owner occupied Private rented	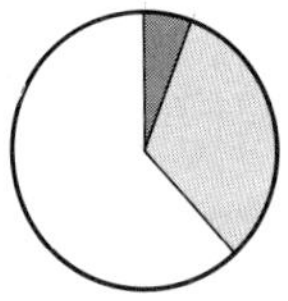	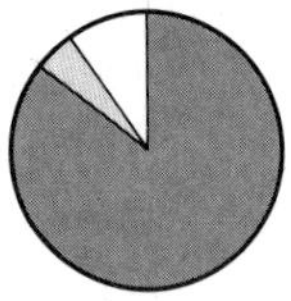	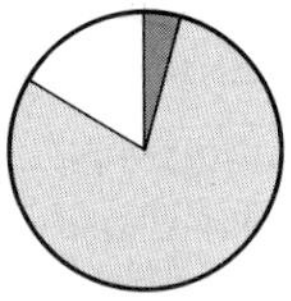	
Socio-economic group Professional/managerial Non manual Skilled manual Semi skilled Unskilled	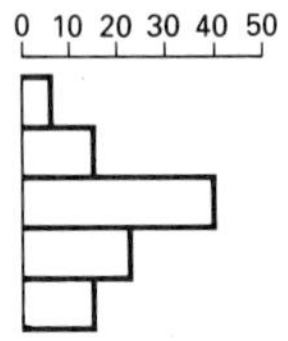	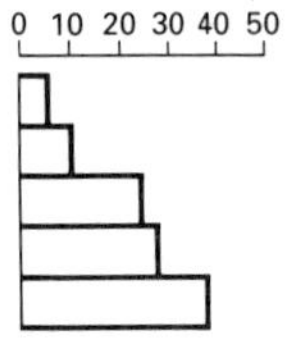	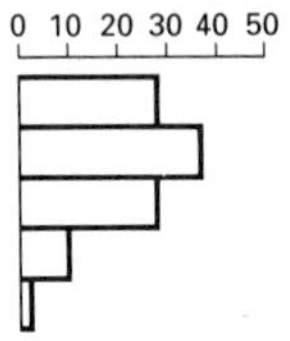	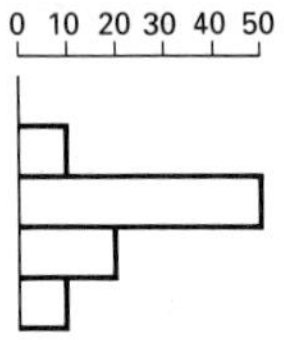
Population structure 60+ 35-59 15-34 0-14	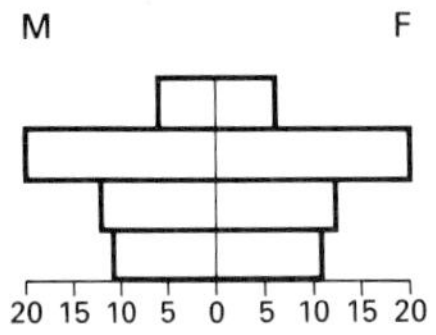	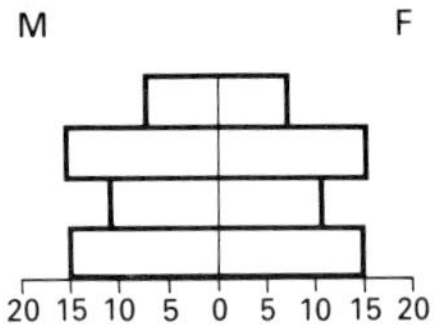	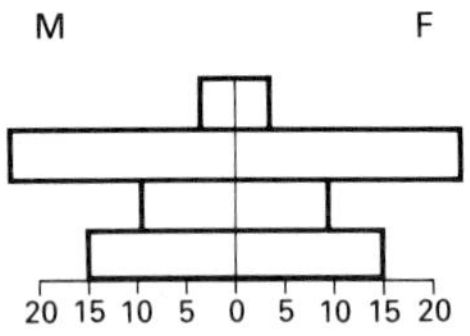	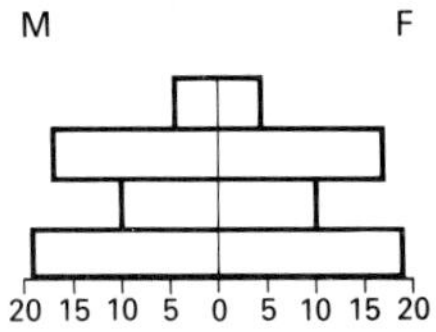
Quality of environment				
% households with WC, hot water	84	96	100	100
% households with garage	0	10	85	5
% more than 1 person per room	24	9	4	20
Other features				
% moving into area in last year	33	6	15	4
% unemployed (1985)	22	28	7	17
% born outside UK	46	3	6	2

RESIDENTIAL ENVIRONMENTS

5 **Refer to pages 60 to 66 in the resource book.**
Study Figures 8g and 8h on the previous page which give some definitions of terms and information about four residential areas.
Answer the following questions using the information in Figures 8g and 8h.

a   Give the names of four different house designs. (2 marks)
b   What is the meaning of the term 'tenure'? (1 mark)
c   What is the name of the graph used to show tenure? (1 mark)
d   What percentage of owner-occupied housing is there in suburbia? (1 mark)
e   What do socio-economic statistics tell you about people? (2 marks)
f   What socio-economic group would a doctor or bank manager be in? (1 mark)
g   What is the name of the graph used in the figure to show socio-economic groups? (1 mark)
h   Which housing area has the most non-manual and professional/managerial workers? (1 mark)
i   Which area has the most skilled and semi-skilled workers? (1 mark)
j   The type of graph used to show population structure is called a **population pyramid**. What two things does it tell ou about population? (2 marks)
k   Which area has the greatest proportion of people younger than 34? (1 mark)

6 **Refer to pages 60 to 66 in the resource book.**
Summarise the characteristics of different residential areas by using one of the following two suggestions.
Use the information in Figures 8g and 8h as well as the descriptions, diagrams and photographs in the resource book.

a   Describe the characteristics of the four main residential area types:
    old inner city   **inner city redevelopment**
    suburbia   **outer city council estate**

   You should include in your writing something on the following:
   Named example, location in city, design and age, tenure, main socio-economic groups, quality of environment, bad points and good points.
   Write half to a full page on each one. (20 marks)

or b Complete the table below (Figure 8i) for each of the four residential area types.
   You should copy the table on to a double page.
   For each box write a sentence or give brief information. (20 marks)

Figure 8i

	Old inner city	Inner city redevelopment	Suburbia	Outer city council estate
Named example				
Location in city				
Design and age				
Tenure				
Main socio-economic groups				
Quality of environment				
Bad points				
Good points				

RESIDENTIAL ENVIRONMENTS

8 Refer to pages 60 and 61 in the resource book.
The photograph in Figure 8j shows part of an old inner city residential area in a typical British city.

Figure 8j
Figure 8k

a i) Make a copy of the photosketch in Figure 8k.
   ii) Add the following labels to the sketch:

   **Terraced housing   Old houses   Front door exits on to street
   No trees or landscaping   Generally well kept appearance
   No garages   Cars parked on street   No gardens**   (8 marks)

   iii) In pencil lightly add colour to the sketch.   (1 mark)
   iv) Add a title to your sketch.   (1 mark)
   v) Write a paragraph to describe the main features shown in the photograph.
       (2 marks)

b What are the advantages of living in an area like this which consists of older housing but is located close to the city centre?   (2 marks)

c Imagine that you have been appointed chief planning officer for an inner city area of a British city.
You are asked to draw up plans to relieve the problems of the area. Suggest how these problems might be reduced.   (10 marks)

9 Study the census information below (Figure 8l) for three residential areas in a large British city.

Figure 8l

Area	Population per sq. km.	Housing Council	Housing Owner occupied	Private Rented	% of families with car	% males unemployed	Pop change 1971-81
1	76	40	17	43	19	28	—38%
2	20	27	65	8	65	9	+8.5%
3	60	76	21	3	32	13	+24%

a i) In which area is the population density highest?   (1 mark)
   ii) In which area is there the greatest population decline?   (1 mark)
   iii) Area 3 is an overspill area where people are being rehoused in new estates mainly built by the local authority.
        Give two pieces of evidence from the table to support this.   (2 marks)

b Area 2 is a modern suburban housing area. Describe the main features of this type of area by using the information in the table and your own knowledge.
Use the following headings:
   i) Likely design of house.
   ii) Characteristics of people living there.
   iii) Advantages of living in this type of area.   (5 marks)

10 Refer to pages 62 and 63 in the resource book.
Study Figure 8m which shows the location of areas with high percentages of local authority (council) housing in a major British city.

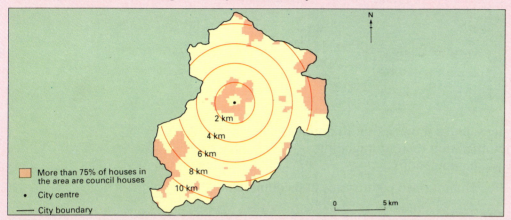

Figure 8m

i) Describe the distribution of council housing shown on the map. Use the distance circles to help you. (2 marks)

ii) 'The council housing has mostly been built since 1948 to allow for urban expansion and redevelopment'.
How does this statement help to explain the pattern you have described? (4 marks)

MEG,A 1988

11 Use pages 60 to 61 and 66 to 67 in the resource book to help you with this question.
The two maps below (Figure 8n) show different areas on the OS Map of Coventry.

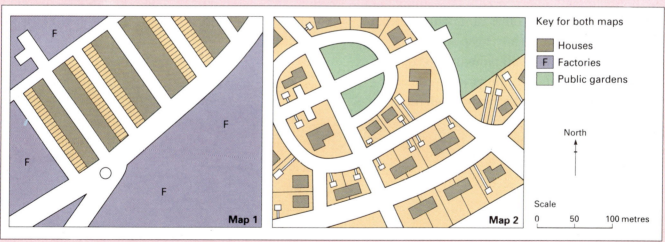

Figure 8n

a Study Map 1. Suggest the possible:
  ■ type of houses,   ■ age of houses. (2 marks)

b Study map 2. Suggest the possible:
  ■ type of houses,   ■ age of houses. (2 marks)

c Comment on the differences between these two housing areas in respect of:
  i) gardens,   ii) car parking,   iii) number of residents. (3 marks)

d Give a four figure grid reference from the OS map (pages 76 and 77) to show where each type of housing might be found.

NEA,(3304) 1989

RESIDENTIAL ENVIRONMENTS

12 **Page 67 of the resource book will help you with this question.**
Study Figure 8o which shows population changes by age group.

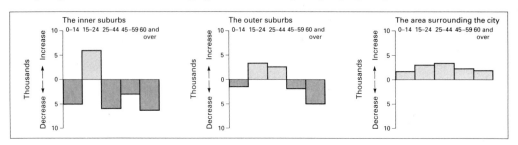

Figure 8o

a i) Which age group in the inner suburbs shows a gain in population? (1 mark)
  ii) Which area has a greater out-migration than in-migration? (1 mark)
  iii) Which area shows an increase in population? (1 mark)

b The area surrounding the city contains open countryside and commuter villages.
  i) What is a commuter village? (1 mark)
  ii) What are the attractions of living in a commuter village? (2 marks)
  iii) What problems may arise in commuter villages due to their rapid increase in size? (3 marks)

13 **Pages 60, 61, 68 and 69 in the resource book will be helpful with this question.**

a Most of the inner city areas in Britain have great housing problems. In order to explain how some of these housing problems have arisen, make a large copy of Figure 8p and put the following statements in the boxes in the diagram in the best order.

- People on low incomes cannot afford repairs.
- Run down houses are cheap so that poorer people live there.
- Houses become even more in need of repairs.
- Old houses built in the nineteenth century.
- In need of repairs and improvement. (4 marks)

Figure 8p

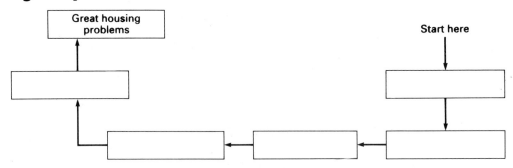

Figure 8q

b i) Some people from old mining settlements and inner city areas have been rehoused in New Towns. With the help of an example (or examples), describe the lay out of British New Towns. (You may refer to housing, industry, shopping, transport, recreation etc.) (8 marks)
  ii) Give one possible reason for the person's view in Figure 8q. (2 marks)

NEA,B 1989

RESIDENTIAL ENVIRONMENTS

14 Refer to pages 68 and 69 in the resource book.

a   Write out the sentences below and fill in the missing spaces with the following words:
planned   overcrowding   1946   industry

New Towns have been a feature of urban development in Britain since _____. Their aim is to relieve _____ in large cities, attract new _____ to areas of unemployment and provide pleasant living conditions in a _____ environment. (4 marks)

b   Study Figure 8r which shows the location of some New Towns.
  i) Make a copy of the map.
  ii) Unscramble the letters to give the names of each New Town. (7 marks)
  iii) In brackets next to each New Town, give the name of a nearby town or city from the following list.
  (One has been done to help you).

  Belfast   Liverpool
  Newcastle   London
  Cardiff   Birmingham
  (6 marks)

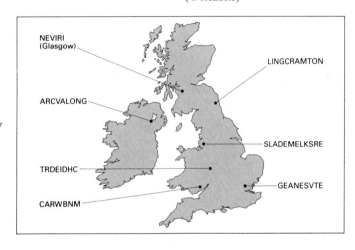

Figure 8r

c   Study Figure 8s which is a sketch map of Stevenage, a typical New Town.
  i) How far is Stevenage from London? (1 mark)
  ii) From the map, give **two** ways in which planners have tried to make traffic flow easier in the New Town. (2 marks)
  iii) From the map, give **two** features that help to improve transport links with other towns. (2 marks)
  iv) Where in the town is industry located? Suggest a reason for this. (3 marks)

d   Describe the main features of a Neighbourhood Unit. (2 marks)

e   What evidence is there from the map to suggest a 'Garden City' environment? (3 marks)

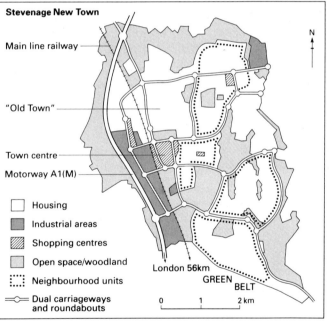

Figure 8s

15 In the last 40 years many people have left Britain's large cities to live in New Towns.

a   Name one New Town and state near which town or city it is located. (1 mark)

b   Describe the main features of its layout. (4 marks)

c   Describe **two** of the main features of the New Town which make it different in layout from an older town.

d   Explain how the quality of the enviroment in the New Town is better than many older city areas.

NINE POPULATION CHANGES

1 Refer to page 70 in the resource book.
Study Figure 9a which shows the UK population 1951 — 2001.

Figure 9a

a Write out and complete the following sentences using one of the suggestions given in the brackets.

i) The graph is an example of a _____ graph. (bar, line, pie).
ii) The population of the UK in 1951 was about _____ million.
(51.0, 50.2, 54.0).
iii) The population of the UK in _____ was about 56.8 million.
(1961, 1976, 1986).
iv) Between 1951 and 1986 the UK's population increased by _____ million.
(2.3, 5.8, 6.6).
v) In the future, it is expected that the UK's population will _____ .
(decrease slowly, remain steady, increase slowly).
(6 marks)

b The population graph is drawn from ten yearly census data and annual estimates.

i) What is a census? (1 mark)
ii) Why is it important to be able to estimate the future population? (2 marks)

2 Refer to page 70 in the resource book.
a i) Make a copy of the graph outline shown in Figure 9b. (1 mark)
ii) Plot the population change information given in Figure 9c as a bar graph. Greater London has been done for you. (4 marks)
iii) Add labels and a suitable title to the graph. (1 mark)
b i) Which place or area has had the greatest population increase during the period? (1 mark)
ii) Which place or area has had the greatest population decrease during the period? (1 mark)
iii) Which of the following statements best describes population changes in the UK between 1971 and 1981? (3 marks)
- Population losses have been mainly in the urban areas.
- Population decline has been mainly in the inaccessible rural areas.
- Population increase has occurred in planned urban environments.
- Population gains have been mainly in conurbations and other urban areas.
- Population gains have been mainly in the countryside and in newly developed areas.

c Suggest how improvements in transport and accessibility may affect where people choose to live. (2 marks)

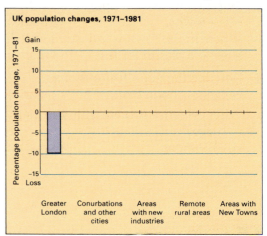

Figure 9b

Figure 9c

Some UK population changes 1971 — 1981	
Greater London	− 10%
Conurbations and other cities	− 8%
Areas with new industries	+ 4%
Remote rural areas	+ 11%
Areas with New Towns	+ 16%

POPULATION CHANGES

3 Refer to page 70 in the resource book.
Study Figures 9b and 9d which show some United Kingdom population changes and suggested reasons for those changes.

Figure 9d

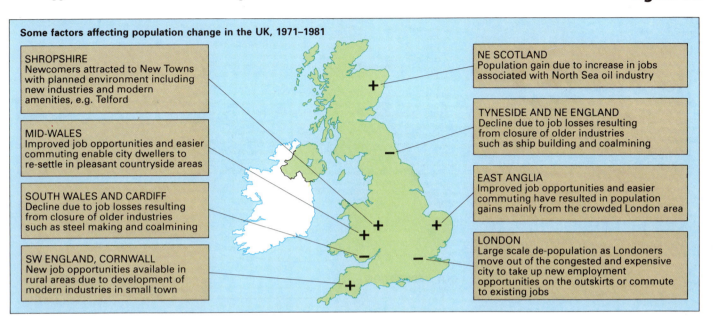

a Make a large copy of the table shown in Figure 9e below.
b Complete the table. Greater London has been done for you. (12 marks)

Figure 9e

Place or area	Change	Named example	Reasons for change
Greater London	10% loss	Inner London and outer suburbs	City expensive and congested. Improved commuting from outskirts. New job opportunities away from city.
Conurbations and other cities			
Areas with new industries			
Remote rural areas			
Areas with New Towns			

4 Pages 67 and 70 in the resource book will help you with this question.

a The table below gives information about the size of population in a small area in the Northern Pennines from 1951 to 1981.

Year	1951	1961	1971	1981
Population	302	252	240	234

  i) In which ten-year period did the population change most? (1 mark)
  ii) Give **two** reasons for the population trend shown in the table. (2 marks)
  iii) Suggest **one** measure which could be taken to stop this trend. (1 mark)

b i) Give **two** reasons for the growth of commuter villages round many of our larger towns and cities. (2 marks)
  ii) State **two** problems sometimes arising as a result of the growth of commuter villages. (2 marks)

NEA, B 1987

POPULATION CHANGES

5 Refer to pages 70 and 74 in the resource book.

Study Figure 9f which shows out-migration from cities to the urban fringe, New Towns, and countryside locations.

Figure 9f

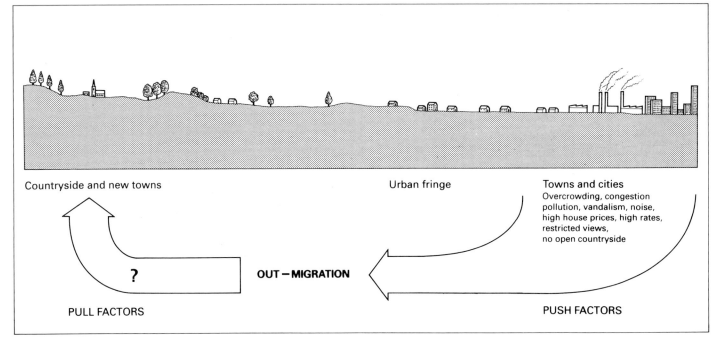

a   What is the meaning of the term 'push factors'? (1 mark)

b i) Name **one** 'pull factor' that makes the rural areas attractive to people from the urban areas. (1 mark)

ii) Which people tend to move out of the inner city areas? Give reasons for your answer. (3 marks)

c i) Why have rural areas in Britain become more attractive to live in during the last ten years or so? (2 marks)

ii) What problems might in-migration cause for rural areas? (2 marks)

6 Refer to pages 72 and 73 in the resource book.

The inner city areas of many cities are old, past their best and are often not very pleasant places in which to live. Urban decay and urban deprivation are common in these areas.

a   Make a copy of the table in Figure 9g and complete it by writing in each of the following terms against the correct descriptions.

Urban decay   **Urban deprivation**   **Conurbation**
Basic amenities (4 marks)

b   Give four methods that may be used to measure urban deprivation. (4 marks)

Figure 9g

Urban term	Definition
	Essential needs in a home, e.g. bathroom, toilet, hot water.
	An area of a town or city that is in decline. Buildings are old and need repair and living conditions are generally poor.
	Areas in towns or cities where people often suffer low living standards with unemployment, poor housing, and low incomes.
	A very large urban area formed when towns or cities merge with each other to form a large built up area.

POPULATION CHANGES

7 Refer to pages 72 and 73 in the resource book.
The Clydeside conurbation in Scotland is an area where urban decay and urban deprivation have been recognised and the problems tackled.

a What were **ten** main problems of the area? (5 marks)

b The renewal project for the area was called GEAR. What do the initials GEAR stand for? (1 mark)

c What was the main reason for the GEAR project being set up? (1 mark)

d Figure 9h shows the six aims of the GEAR project.
 i) Make a large copy of Figure 9h.
 ii) For each aim, add a descriptive sentence and an actual example to show what has been done. (5 marks)

e What successes have been achieved by the GEAR project? (2 marks)

f What problems slowed down progress for GEAR in the 1980s? (2 marks)

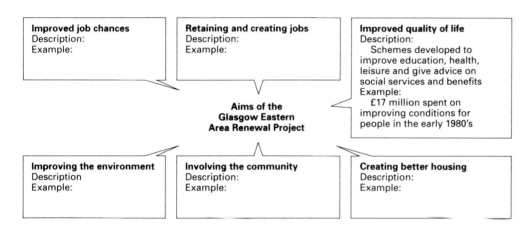

Figure 9h

8 Refer to page 74 in the resource book, and to Figure 9i.
Write out the terms from List one and add the correct definitions from List two.
(6 marks)

List one

- Migrant
- Emigrant
- Immigrant
- Old Commonwealth
- New Commonwealth
- Ethnic minority

List two

- A person who leaves one place or country to settle in another.
- Someone who has been allowed to enter a country with the intention of living there.
- Groups of people with a common identity, e.g. Similar cultural beliefs, social organisation, religion etc.
- Countries settled by British immigrants some time ago, e.g. Australia, Canada, New Zealand.
- A person who is moving home from one place or country to another.
- Countries such as India, Bangladesh, the West Indies and some African countries that are or were part of the Commonwealth.

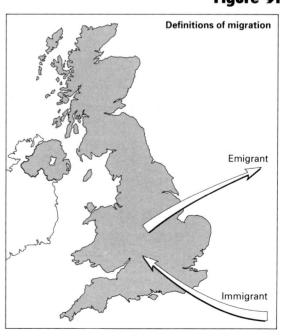

Figure 9i

9 Refer to pages 74 and 75 in the resource book.
Study Figure 9j which shows the origin of migrants accepted for settlement into the United Kingdom in 1988.

a What is meant by the term, 'Old Commonwealth' countries? (1 mark)

b Name **two** New Commonwealth countries. (2 marks)

c Which area was the origin of most migrants in 1986? (1 mark)

d Why were immigrants encouraged to come to Britain after the Second World War? (1 mark)

e Suggest three problems that immigrants may have when they settle in a new country? (3 marks)

Origins of immigrants to UK, 1988
New Commonwealth Countries 48%
Others 27%
Old Commonwealth Countries 14%
Europe 11%

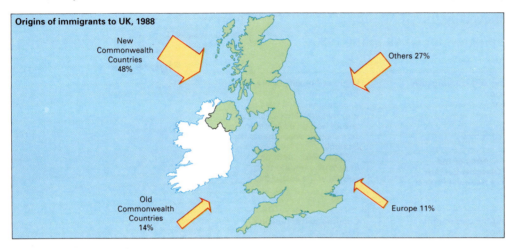

Figure 9j

10 Refer to pages 74 and 75 in the resource book.
Study the information in Figure 9k which shows some features of immigrants and ethnic groups in Britain.

Figure 9k

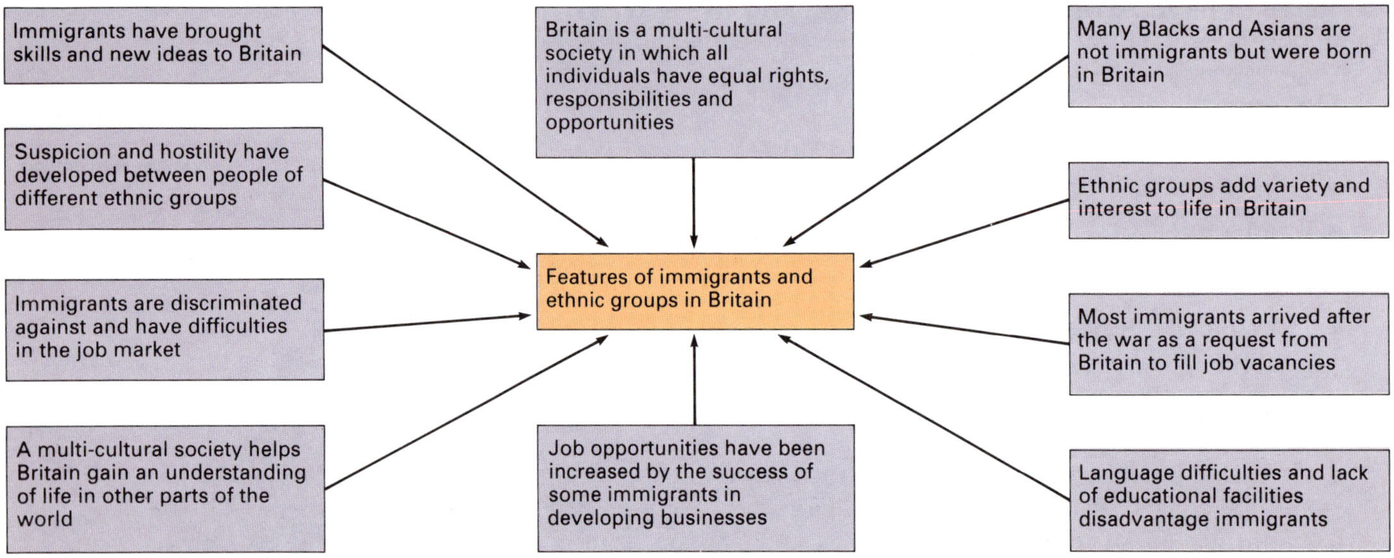

Features of immigrants and ethnic groups in Britain
Immigrants have brought skills and new ideas to Britain
Britain is a multi-cultural society in which all individuals have equal rights, responsibilities and opportunities
Many Blacks and Asians are not immigrants but were born in Britain
Suspicion and hostility have developed between people of different ethnic groups
Ethnic groups add variety and interest to life in Britain
Immigrants are discriminated against and have difficulties in the job market
Most immigrants arrived after the war as a request from Britain to fill job vacancies
A multi-cultural society helps Britain gain an understanding of life in other parts of the world
Job opportunities have been increased by the success of some immigrants in developing businesses
Language difficulties and lack of educational facilities disadvantage immigrants

a Make a copy of the table. You will need about half a page.

b Complete the table by writing the statements from Figure 9k in the correct columns. (11 marks)

c Give your table a title. (1 mark)

Facts	Benefits	Problems

POPULATION CHANGES

11 Refer to pages 74 and 75 in the resource.

Study Figures 9l and 9m which give information about some wards in Birmingham.

Figure 9l

Ward	Distance from centre	% of New Commonwealth families	% Unemployed	Professional or managerial occupations	Skilled or semi-skilled workers
1 Aston	2 km	36.8	35.1	4.1	43.1
2 Gravelly Hill	7 km	11.7	22.9	11.2	29.8
3 Handsworth	4 km	38.2	36.5	6.1	40.5
4 Northfield	12 km	2.2	14.2	14.0	24.0
5 Small Heath	3 km	31.9	30.6	6.4	39.9
6 Sutton Coldfield	14 km	1.2	8.7	50.2	6.8

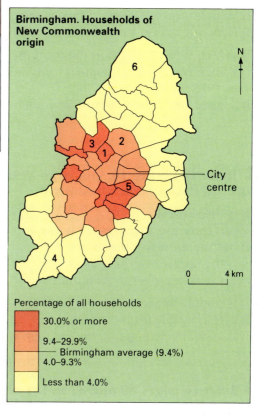

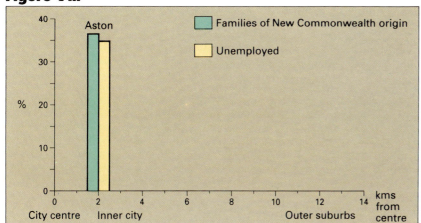

Figure 9m

a i) Make a copy of the graph outline given in Figure 9m.
  ii) Complete the graph using information from Figure 9l. (10 marks)
  iii) Add labels and a title to the graph. (3 marks)

b i) Which **two** wards have the highest percentage of families of New Commonwealth origin? (2 marks)
  ii) Which wards are less than 5 km from the city centre? (3 marks)
  iii) Write a sentence to describe how the proportion of New Commonwealth families changes with distance from the city centre. (1 mark)
  iv) Which of the following statements best describes the general location of the wards with a high proportion of families of New Commonwealth origin?
  (1 mark)

- On the edge of the city.
- Scattered throughout the city.
- Close to the city centre.
- Mainly to the west of the city centre.

c Using information from your graph, (Figure 9n), and from the resource book, suggest reasons for the distribution of New Commonwealth families in Birmingham. (4 marks)

d For a town or city that you have studied other than Birmingham:
  i) Name the town or city.
  ii) Describe the distribution of the ethnic population. (2 marks)
  iii) Suggest reasons for this distribution using actual examples where possible.
  (4 marks)

TEN TRANSPORT

1 Refer to Figure 10.4 on page 79 in the resource book.

a i) Which form of transport carried most passengers in the 1950s?
ii) Which form of transport carried most passengers in the 1980s?
iii) Give one reason for the change between **a** i) and **a** ii). (3 marks)

b i) Which type of transport did most men use to get to work in 1975-76?
ii) Which was the least popular form of transport used by women to reach work in 1975-76?
iii) Suggest one reason why more women than men walked to work in 1975-76. (6 marks)

2 Refer to Figure 10.5 on page 79 in the resource book.
Which of the four types of transport:

a i) is the slowest,
ii) can carry most passengers at one go,
iii) has the most flexible routes,
iv) is the fastest over long distances,
v) is the fastest over short distances,

b i) is responsible for most congestion,
ii) is responsible for most pollution,
iii) is least affected by fog, ice and high winds? (8 marks)

3 Refer to pages 80 and 81 in the resource book.
The graph below (Figure 10a) shows the average daily traffic flow between a large city and a nearby commuter town.

a i) Which was the time of day with the lowest traffic flow:
0400 hours, 0800 hours or midnight?
ii) Was the number of vehicles on the road at that time:
100, 1500 or none? (2 marks)

b i) At what time is the peak flow?
ii) Why are there two peak flows in a day?
iii) Why is there a small peak flow at about 1200 hours (noon)?
iv) Why is there another small peak flow about 2200 hours? (4 marks)

c List **four** traffic problems that might occur in the large city as a result of the morning peak flow. (4 marks)

d i) Name **two** schemes which the large city may have introduced to try to solve these traffic problems. (2 marks)
ii) Give **two** advantages and **two** disadvantages for each of the two schemes which you have named. (8 marks)

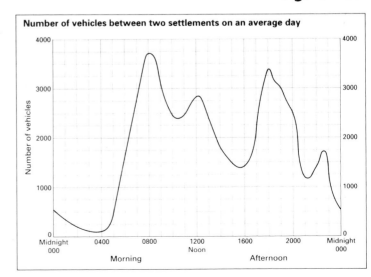

Figure 10a

TRANSPORT

4 **Refer to page 81 in the resource book.**
The two maps, Figure 10b, show a city centre somewhere in Britain. The first map was of the city centre in 1970, the second in 1990.

a i) Which of the following describes where most shops and offices were located in 1970:

- along main roads,
- mostly along one main road,
- scattered all over the city centre?

ii) What traffic and environmental problems might have occurred in the city centre in 1970? (3 marks)

b i) Describe **four** changes which had been made by 1990 to try to solve the problems which you listed in **a** ii). (4 marks)

ii) Name **two** groups in the local community who may have benefitted from the changes and **two** groups who were opposed to the changes. Give reasons for your answer. (4 marks)

Figure 10b

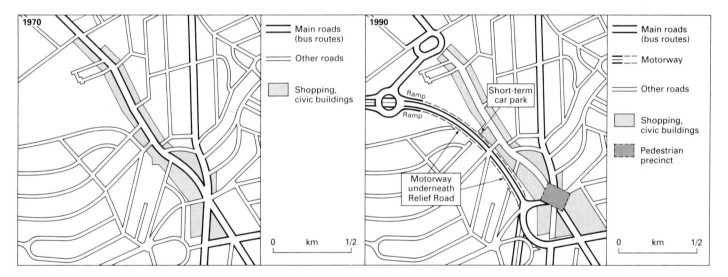

5 **Refer to page 82 of the resource book.**

a i) Copy out the table below. Tick the appropriate column to show which groups of people were likely to have been in favour of the M25, and which groups against it.

ii) In each case give a reason for your answer. (7 marks)

b Would you have been in favour or against the M25? Give two reasons for your answer. (2 marks)

Figure 10c

Group	For	Against	Reason
People living in houses alongside the new motorway			
Firms in towns north of London sending goods by road to places south			
People living in central London on streets used by heavy lorries			
Farmers whose land will be crossed by the motorway			
Firms in central London sending goods by road to the rest of Britain and the EC			
Hospitals and traffic police in the middle of London			
Building workers			

TRANSPORT

6 **Page 83 and Figure 10.17 in the resource book will help you with this question.**
Study the flow diagram below (Figure 10d) showing how private and public transport in towns affect each other together with the table which shows the missing phrases from the flow diagram.

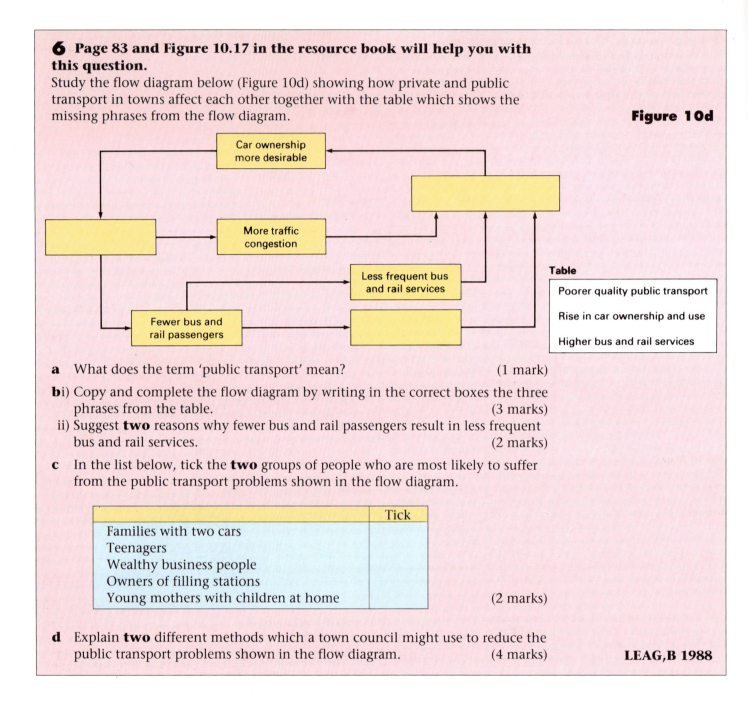

Figure 10d

a What does the term 'public transport' mean? (1 mark)

b i) Copy and complete the flow diagram by writing in the correct boxes the three phrases from the table. (3 marks)
ii) Suggest **two** reasons why fewer bus and rail passengers result in less frequent bus and rail services. (2 marks)

c In the list below, tick the **two** groups of people who are most likely to suffer from the public transport problems shown in the flow diagram.

	Tick
Families with two cars	
Teenagers	
Wealthy business people	
Owners of filling stations	
Young mothers with children at home	

(2 marks)

d Explain **two** different methods which a town council might use to reduce the public transport problems shown in the flow diagram. (4 marks)

LEAG,B 1988

7 **Refer to the Ordnance Survey map of Coventry on pages 76 and 77.**

a i) Name **three** types of transport (past or present) that can be found in grid square 3380.
ii) What is the six figure map reference for Coventry's main line railway station? (4 marks)

b You have to give a visitor to Coventry instructions on how to reach the railway station from the M6 motorway. Rewrite the following paragraph choosing the correct instruction from each alternative in brackets.
(Leave the M6 at junction (2/3) and take the (A4/A46) road. After (5/15 km) you come to a roundabout in (Wyken/Church End). Turn (left/right) and continue until you reach the (inner/outer) ring road. Go in an (clockwise/anticlockwise) direction and take the (first/second) main road to the (right/left). The station is on the (right/left) hand side of the road. The station is to the (north/south) of the city centre. (10 marks)

8 Refer to pages 88-89 in the resource book.

Figure 10e shows the percentage change in the value of trade for eight English ports between 1970 and 1980.

a From the map:
 i) Name the port in which there had been the greatest percentage increase in trade between 1970 and 1980.
 ii) Name the port in which there had been the greatest percentage decrease in trade between 1970 and 1980.
 iii) State the main difference in location between those ports which had increased their trade and those ports which had shown a decrease between 1970 and 1980. (3 marks)

b In what ways has the location of the ports helped to explain the increases in trade? (2 marks)

c The ports with an increase in trade often have roll-on/roll-off facilities. What is meant by roll-on/roll-off facilities? (2 marks)

d Why are some English ports expecting to face greater competition for both cargoes and passengers after 1992? (1 mark)

NEA, B 1989

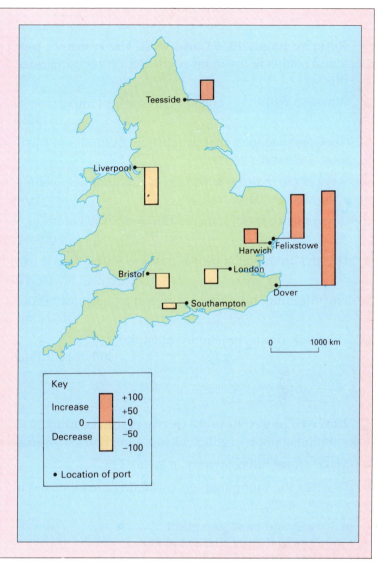

Figure 10e

Figure 10f

9 You will need to refer to Figure 10.29 on page 88 of the resource book.

The photograph (Figure 10f) shows part of the port at Tilbury.

The jetty labelled A on the photograph is the black L-shaped feature on the left of the resource book map.

a i) What is being unloaded at the jetty?
 ii) What is being stored in building B?
 iii) What is being stored at C awaiting to be loaded onto a ship?
 iv) What is River D called?
 v) What are the buildings at E called?
 vi) What type of transport is found at F? (6 marks)

b Name **two** sea areas to which the arrow at G is pointing. (2 marks)

c Is the photograph taken with the camera facing a NE, SE, SW, or a NW direction? (1 mark)

ELEVEN SHOPPING

1 Refer to pages 90, 91 and 98 in the resource book.
Copy and complete the following sentences by using **one** of the suggestions in the brackets.

a   Where something is organised in order of importance it is called a _____
(shopping centre **or** hierarchy).

b   Goods are products that people buy. Examples of these would be shops selling food, TV's and _____ (holidays **or** clothing).

c   Services are facilities which are useful to or help people. Examples of these are a launderette, bank and _____ (shoe shop **or** hairdresser).

d   Convenience shops sell everyday goods such as bread, milk and _____
(newspapers **or** garden tools).

e   The area from which people travel to visit a shop is called a _____
(trade area **or** hierarchy).

f   The minimum number of people in a trade area needed to support a good or service is called the _____ (range **or** threshold population).

g   The trade area is sometimes called the _____
(sphere of influence **or** location factor).

(7 marks)

2 Refer to pages 90 to 97 in the resource book.
Information about four different shopping types is given below.

a   Make a large full page copy of Figure 11a.

b   Describe the shopping types by adding the following information to the correct boxes. (5 marks)

- Largest and most important shopping district situated in city centre.
- Groups of 5 to 20 shops mainly located in large housing estates.
- Very large shops or new shopping developments located on the edge of the city.
- Small shops on their own selling convenience goods.
- A line of shops along a main road leading to the city centre.

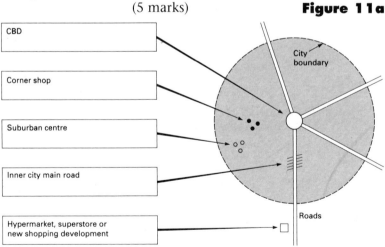

Figure 11a

3 Refer to pages 90 to 93 and page 98 in the resource book.
Copy and complete the paragraph below using the following words.

department   trading area   main   goods   centre   services

The Central Business District is the _____ shopping area. It is found in the _____ of a town at the junction of main roads and has a very large _____ . It provides a wide range of _____ including all sorts of food, clothing and specialist shops and also has many _____ such as banking, building societies and insurance. Large _____ stores and nationwide supermarkets are also found in the CBD.

58

4 Refer to page 90 in the resource book.
When something is organised in order of importance it is called a **hierarchy**.

a i) Draw the pyramid diagram (Figure 11b) showing a school hierarchy. Add the following terms next to the correct arrow:

Teacher   Deputy head
Headteacher
Head of department   (4 marks)

ii) Add the name of someone from school to each level of the hierarchy.
(4 marks)

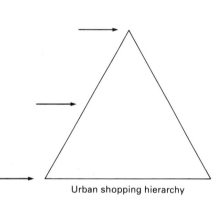

Figure 11b — School hierarchy

Figure 11c — Urban shopping hierarchy

b Types of shopping area can also be organised in a hierarchy.
The term 'order' is used to describe how important a centre is. High order centres are the largest and have the greatest choice of goods and services.

Low order centres are small and tend to supply a range of day to day needs with little choice.

i) Draw the pyramid diagram (Figure 11c) showing an urban shopping hierarchy. Add the following terms next to the correct arrows:

Middle order centre
Low order centre
High order centre   (3 marks)

ii) Add the name of a shopping centre in your area for each level of the hierarchy.   (3 marks)

iii) Use the two word searches below to complete the following table. (The words read across and downwards. There are ten words in each wordsearch).
(10 marks)

Some features, goods and services of shopping centres	
Low order centres	High order centres

Low order centres

```
S O R H S B M I L K Z
M T S E P R V O N F R
Q C O R N E R S H O P
I L U P T A O W N O L
L U P Z R D B E C D O
N E W S P A P E R S C
D F G T Q I J T N K A
P O T A T O E S S O L
```

High order centres

```
S S P E C I A L I S T
H L Z D B Y W X V M C
O A Q R A C B D A L H
E F U R N I T U R E O
S E P O K H G N I K I
I N S U R A N C E F C
D C I T Y C E N T R E
K O B I G O E B Y A T
```

c i) What is a hierarchy?   (1 mark)
ii) Write a paragraph to describe what is meant by a high order centre. (2 marks)
iii) Write a paragraph to describe what is meant by a low order centre.   (2 marks)

SHOPPING

5 Refer to pages 90 to 99 in the resource book.
Summarise the characteristics of different shopping types by using **one** of the following two suggestions:

a Describe the characteristics of the four main shopping types: (20 marks)
- CBD.
- Corner shop.
- Suburban centre.
- Hypermarket.

i) You should write between a half and a full page on each one.
ii) You should include in your writing something on the following: main features, location, date when built, type of goods available, trade area, distance shoppers travel, frequency of visits, method of travel.
iii) For a town or city that you know, give named examples for each of the four shopping types you have described.

OR

b Complete a star diagram for each of the shopping types: (20 marks)
- CBD.
- Corner shop.
- Suburban centre.
- Hypermarket.

i) For each shopping type, make a full page copy of Figure 11d.
ii) For each box in the star diagram write the title as given then add the correct information from the choices given below.
iii) **Print** in block letters because you are constructing a diagram.
iv) Add colour to make the diagram easier to understand and more interesting to look at.
v) For a town or city that you know, give named examples for each of the four shopping types you have described.

Figure 11d

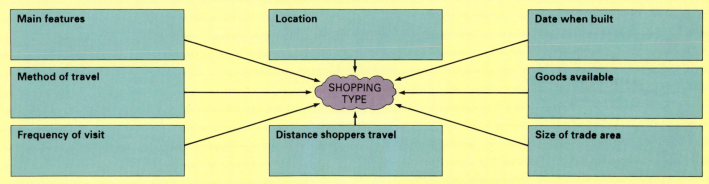

6 Pages 90 to 99 in the resource book will help you to answer the question.
Study Figure 11e below.

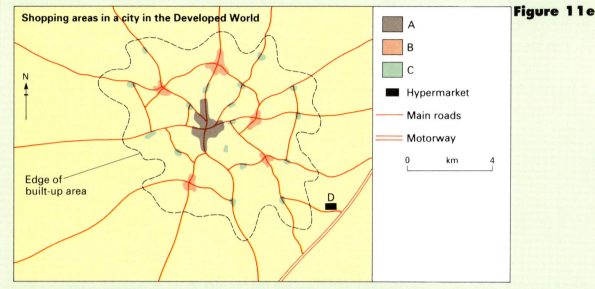

Figure 11e

a i) Describe the location of the hypermarket shown on the map.
ii) Name **two** groups of people who are likely to have objected to the building of the hypermarket. For **each** group, give a reason for their objections.
(7 marks)

b i) State **two** differences you would find between the types of shops found in the areas marked A and C.
ii) Why are there more shopping areas of type B than A? (4 marks)

c Imagine that you are to open a new fashion clothes shop for young people.
i) In which of the centres, A, type B, type C or D would you locate your shop? Give reasons for your answer.
ii) What disadvantages would there be in your chosen location? (6 marks)

d In the centre of many large cities large, covered, air-conditioned shopping centres have been built. For a named example of such a centre:
i) Describe the advantages of the centre for
   a the shopper and   **b** the shopkeeper;
ii) Explain why the shopping centre was built:
- Name of shopping centre.
- Advantages for **a** shopper and **b** shopkeeper.
- Why it was built.
(8 marks)

LEAG,B 1987

---

7 Refer to page 95 of the resource book. Study the Ordnance Survey map of Coventry on pages 76 and 77 for this question.

There are plans to build a superstore at 345757.

a Give **two** reasons why this is a good place for a superstore. (2 marks)

b What effect is its opening likely to have on:
i) a family with a car living in Canley (3077)? (2 marks)
ii) a family without a car living in Hillfields (3479)? (2 marks)

MEG,E 1988

SHOPPING

8 Refer to page 90 in the resource book.

Study Figure 11f which is a cross-section through a typical British city.

a Make a copy of Figure 11f.

b Show the location of the various shopping types by printing the following information in the correct boxes. (6 marks)

- Central Business District shopping area
- Inner city corner shops
- Outer suburb shopping parades
- Outer suburb corner shops
- Inner city main road shopping area
- Hypermarket or Superstore

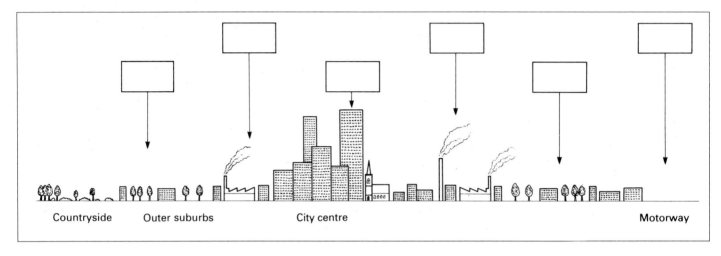

Figure 11f

9 Refer to pages 90, 96 and 97 in the resource book.

Study the information in Figure 11g which gives the views of some local residents about the closure of their corner shop.

a From the comments made by local people, give **three** advantages of corner shops. (3 marks)

b Suggest **two** reasons why some corner shops are closing down. (2 marks)

c Imagine that a corner shop that you often use is about to close down. Write a letter to your local newspaper giving your views as to why shops like this should remain open if possible.
Your letter should be about 200 words in length. (10 marks)

Figure 11g

10 Refer to pages 92 to 99 in the resource book.
Study Figure 11h which shows the trading areas of Exeter

a What is meant by a trading area (sphere of influence)? (2 marks)

b Which shop has the smallest trading area? (1 mark)

c Which two of the following types of service/shops have the largest trading areas?
**supermarket
chemist
theatre
furniture store
department store** (2 marks)

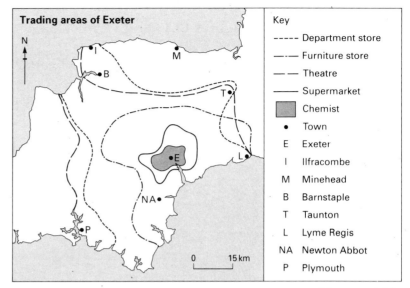

Figure 11h

d How will the shopping pattern change in the Exeter area if a new hypermarket (superstore) is built near Newton Abbot? (2 marks)

e Suggest **three** reasons why out of town hypermarkets (superstores) have become popular in the last 15 years. (3 marks)

f To compete with these out of town centres, many town centres have been pedestrianised and made into precincts.
Explain the advantages and disadvantages of pedestrian precincts. (6 marks)

NEA,C 1988

11 Refer to pages 92 to 99 in the resource book.
Study Figure 11i which gives information about shopping trips in a large British city.

Figure 11i

Shopping centres	Shopping for:				Distance travelled (km)				
	Food	Clothes	Household	Specialist	Up to 1	1—2	2—4	4—10	10+
Corner shop	91	1	2	2	95	2	2	1	0
Suburban centre	89	2	2	2	84	10	4	2	0
CBD	60	24	7	5	6	9	43	37	5
Hypermarket	68	12	17	3	9	13	23	47	8

a Name a specialist shop. (1 mark)

b From which shopping centres do shoppers purchase the greatest variety of goods? (2 marks)

c To which shopping centres do over 75% of the shoppers travel more than 2 km? (2 marks)

d Explain why hypermarkets are located on the outskirts of cities. (2 marks)

e Suggest why hypermarkets attract more short distance shoppers than the CBD (1 mark)

f Which type of shopping centre would be best for a family doing their once weekly shop? Give reasons for your answer. (3 marks)

g Describe and suggest reasons for the likely trade areas served by any **two** of the four types of shopping centre referred to in the table. (4 marks)

TWELVE RECREATION AND TOURISM

1 Refer to an atlas and Figures 12.13 and 12.14 on page 104 of the resource book.

The map (Figure 12a) shows the location of eight British holiday resorts.

  i) Rearrange the jumbled letters to name the eight resorts.
  ii) Match up the name of each resort with its number on the map. (8 marks)
  iii) Copy and complete the following table by linking the eight resorts with the eight descriptive points in Figure 12b. (8 marks)

Figure 12a

Examples of British holiday resorts (not in order)

LACKBLOOP
KORY
BAYTOR
RIGHTBON
KEELDIR
EBIDNURGH
MOREAVIE
ILEHLLWP

Figure 12b

A long stay resort in the West Country	
A day trip resort in South-east England	
A cultural/historic resort in Scotland	
A holiday camp in Wales	
A cultural/historic resort in Yorkshire and Humberside	
A day trip resort in North-west England	
A winter resort in Scotland	
A water sports centre in Northumbria	

2 Study Figures 12.1 and 12.2 on page 100 of the resource book which give information about the distribution of open space in London Boroughs.

 a The partly completed graph (Figure 12c) shows the relationship between open space and distance from the city centre for eight of the ten London Boroughs located on the cross section W — E on Figure 12.2 in the resource book.

  i) Copy and complete the graph by plotting the location of:
     1 Ealing, 2 City of Westminster.
  ii) Label on your graph the London Boroughs marked X and Y. (4 marks)
  iii) Draw in a 'best fit' straight line (you may find Figure 12.4 on page 100 a help).

 b Complete the following passage by selecting the correct word from each pair in the brackets:

 The completed graph shows that the boroughs which are nearest to the city centre have (less/more) open space per 1000 people. This is because land values in the city centre are (low/high) and so it is too (cheap/expensive) to leave land as open space. It is more profitable to use land in the centre for (offices/parks). The borough which least fits this trend is (Tower Hamlets/Westminster).

 This is because _____ . (6 marks)

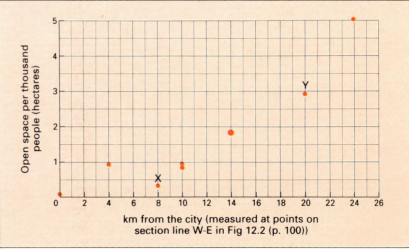

Figure 12c

RECREATION AND TOURISM

3 **Refer to pages 101 and 102 in the resource book.**

a Figure 12d shows the distribution of public open space in five wards of a large industrial town.

Figure 12d

WARD	A	B	C	D	E
Distance from city centre (km)	1.5	3.0	4.5	6.0	7.5
Recreation grounds	2	6	4	2	6
Small parks	1	1	3	2	1
Large parks	0	0	0	1	4
Woodlands	0	0	0	0	2

  i) What is meant by the term 'public open space'? (1 mark)
  ii) Describe and suggest one reason for the distribution of **each** type of public open space shown in Figure 12d. (4 marks)

b Figure 12e shows the distribution of leisure amenities in the same five wards.

Figure 12e

WARD	A	B	C	D	E
Distance from city centre (km)	1.5	3.0	4.5	6.0	7.5
Skating rink	0	1	0	0	0
Bingo hall	4	3	1	0	0
Cinema	4	1	0	0	0
Swimming pool	1	0	0	0	1

  i) What is meant by the term 'leisure amenity'? (1 mark)
  ii) Describe and suggest one reason for the distribution of **each** type of leisure amenity shown in Figure 12e. (4 marks)

c i) Figure 12f below shows the location, in the same city, of a football league ground, a night club/disco, and a sports centre.

Suggest **two** reasons for the location of each amenity. (6 marks)

  ii) The map also shows the location of two public parks (X and Y). Describe, with the help of Figure 12.7 on page 101, how they are likely to differ in terms of:

    1 size,
    2 recreational facilities provided,
    3 distance people are likely to travel,
    4 length of stay of the visitors,
    5 times of the day and/or week with most visitors. (5 marks)

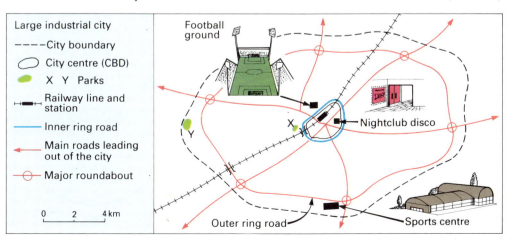

Figure 12f

4 Refer to Figure 12.18 on page 105 in the resource book.

Make the 'Blockbusters gold run' in Figure 12g by solving the following clues to get a linking pattern of hexagons across the puzzle.

- National Parks: S, E, PD, N, LD, YD, D, PC, NYM and BB
- Other special protected areas: NF and NB.
- National scenic areas in Scotland: LL and CM.
- Areas of Outstanding Natural Beauty in Northern Ireland: M and A.
- Long Distance Routes: ODP, WHW, PW and NDW.

(5 marks for a line or 20 total)

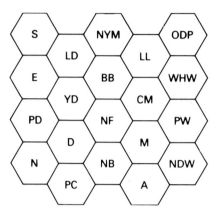

Figure 12g

5 Refer to Figure 12.19 on page 106 in the resource book.

a i) What percentage of people took a holiday in 1977?
ii) What percentage of people took two or more holidays in 1988?
iii) Give **three** reasons for the increase in numbers taking two holidays a year.
(5 marks)

b The completed percentage bar graph (Figure 12h) shows the location of holidays in Britain in 1987.
 i) Make a copy of the second graph and complete it using the figures for 1988 from Figure 12.19b on page 106 of the resource book. (6 marks)
ii) Give **two** differences between 1987 and 1988. (2 marks)

c i) The pie graph for 1951 (Figure 12i) shows the percentages of people using different types of transport to reach their holiday destination. Copy and complete the graph by labelling the types of transport (Figure 12.19c)
(4 marks)
ii) Draw your own pie graph to show the main types of transport used in 1988.
(4 marks)
iii) Account for the differences between the two graphs. (2 marks)

d Figure 12.19d on page 106 shows types of accommodation used by people on holiday in Britain. Choose one illustrative method of showing the figures for 1988 (Do not use a histogram, bar chart or pie graph). (3 marks)

Figure 12h   **Figure 12i**

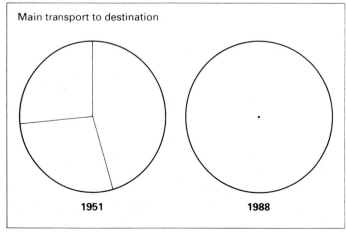

RECREATION AND TOURISM

6 Refer to page 107 in the resource book.
Study the bar graph (Figure 12j) giving information about delegates at Blackpool conferences.

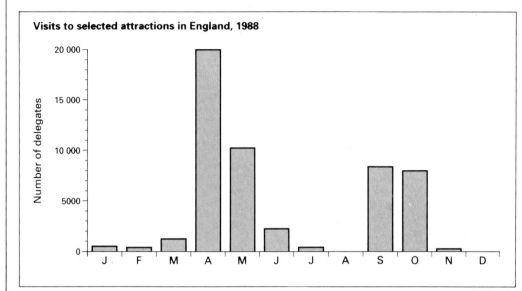

Figure 12j

a   Name the month in which there are most conference delegates at Blackpool.
(1 mark)

b   Give one reason why July and August are of little importance for conferences.
(1 mark)

c   With over a quarter of its workforce employed in the holiday industry Blackpool has problems of unemployment at certain times of the year. In which season is there likely to be the highest unemployment?   (1 mark)

d   State **two** measures (other than attracting conference delegates) taken by Blackpool to reduce seasonal unemployment.   (2 marks)

NEA, B Specimen paper

---

7 The information in Figure 12k was issued by the British Tourist Authority and shows how many visits were made to the more popular tourist locations in Britain in 1988.

Figure 12k

HISTORIC BUILDINGS AND GARDENS	1988 VISITS
Tower of London	2,182,000
Kew Royal Botanic Gardens	1,181,000
Roman Baths and Pump Room, Bath	954,000
Windsor Castle State Apartments	700,000
Warwick Castle	645,000
Stonehenge	640,000
Hampton Court Palace	533,000
MUSEUMS AND ART GALLERIES	
British Museum, London	3,839,000F
National Gallery, London	3,228,000F
Science Museum, London	2,436,000F
Tate Gallery, London	1,581,000F
Natural History Museum, London	1,367,000
Victoria & Albert Museum, London	997,000F
WILDLIFE ATTRACTIONS	
London Zoo	1,326,000
Royal Windsor Safari Park	951,000
Chester Zoo	897,000
Bristol Zoo	572,000
OTHER ATTRACTIONS	
Madame Tussaud's, London	2,705,000
Alton Towers, Staffordshire	2,510,000
Blackpool Tower	1,478,000
Thorpe Park, Surrey	1,028,000
Jorvik Viking Centre, York	866,000

Attractions marked 'F' offer entry free of charge

a i) Rank in order the top six attractions in 1988.   (6 marks)
   ii) How many of those six are in London?   (4 marks)
   iii) Give **three** reasons why the British Museum is the most visited attraction.   (3 marks)

b   Many resorts and tourist attractions gain visitors by advertising. Choose any resort or attraction that you have visited and design a poster which might lead to an increase in tourists/visitors.   (5 marks)

THIRTEEN COMPETITION FOR LAND

1 **Refer to page 108 in the resource book.**
Study Figure 13a which is a model for land use values in a typical British city.

Figure 13a

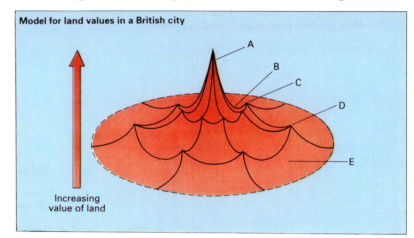

a i) Which of the locations A, B, C, D or E is the city centre?
 ii) Where is the highest land value?
 iii) Where is the lowest land value?
 (3 marks)

b Which of the following is a correct statement about the lines which give shape to the model? (3 marks)
Give a reason for your answer.
- They separate different land uses.
- They mark boundaries within the city.
- They indicate where main roads are most likely to be.

c Copy and complete Figure 13b below by adding the following information to the correct spaces.
- Outer suburbs
- Edge of CBD
- Housing
- accessibility
- Non profit land users with accessibility not so important
- Major crossroads
- Smaller shopping centres
- Offices and shops
- Greatest accessibility.

Figure 13b

LOCATION	LAND USE	REASON
A CBD		
B	Low profit services	Need good assessibility but not able to pay high rates
C	Inner city shops and offices	
D Outer city		Accessible to local area
E		

2 **Refer to pages 58 and 109 in the resource book.**
Study Figure 13c which shows 'green planning' in a typical city.

Figure 13c

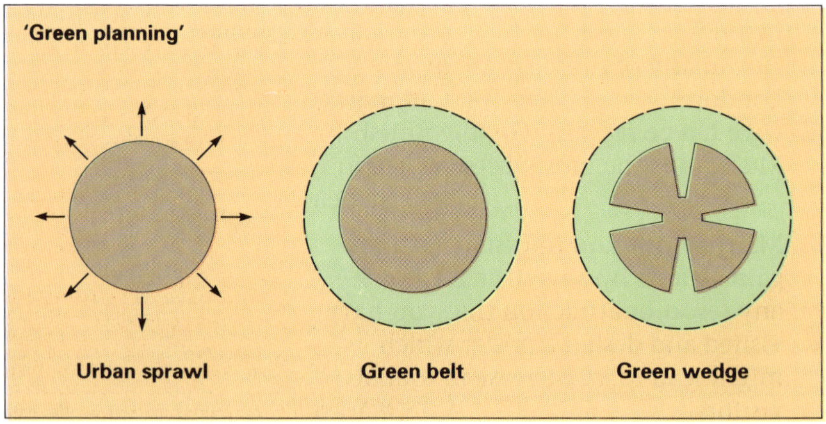

a Make a copy of the three diagrams in Figure 13c

b What is urban sprawl? (1 mark)

c i) What is a green belt? (1 mark)
 ii) What is the purpose of green belts? (2 marks)
 iii) Give **three** types of development which make it difficult to keep green belts? (3 marks)

d i) What are green wedges? (1 mark)
 ii) What are the advantages of green wedges? (2 marks)

COMPETITION FOR LAND

3 Refer to the resource book pages 20 to 23 and 108 to 109.

Since 1980 many new housing estates have been built in England. The diagram (Figure 13d) shows what the land was used for before the estates were built.

a i) Make a copy of the diagram and key.
  ii) Complete the diagram and key to show the following facts:

  > 7% of the land was formerly arable land, and 6% was formerly rough pasture.

  iii) Explain what is meant by the following terms.
  - Arable land,
  - Rough pasture. (4 marks)

b i) Which type of land was most commonly built on?
  ii) Suggest two reasons for this fact. (3 marks)

c Nearly two thirds of the new housing estates were built on former farmland or countryside. Explain why many environmental groups are concerned about this. (3 marks)

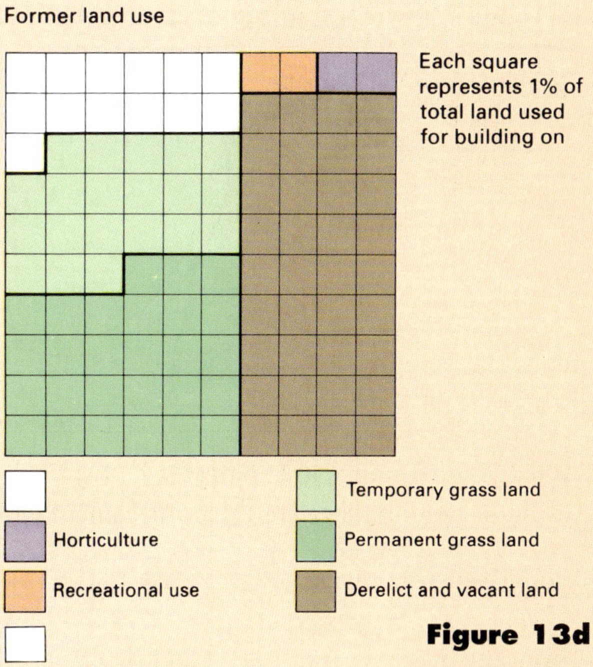

Former land use

Each square represents 1% of total land used for building on

Key: Horticulture, Recreational use, Temporary grass land, Permanent grass land, Derelict and vacant land

Figure 13d
NEA,D 1989

4 Refer to pages 110 and 111 in the resource book.

Study Figure 13e which gives information about National Parks in England and Wales.

a What is a National Park?

b Copy out and complete the following sentences using one of the choices given in the brackets. (3 marks)

 i) The number of National Parks in England and Wales is _____ (ten/eight).
 ii) Most National Parks are located in the _____ (south and east/north and west).
 iii) The three Welsh National Parks are Snowdonia, Pembrokeshire coast and _____ (Exmoor/Brecon Beacons). (3 marks)

c i) Which **three** National Parks have the most people within three hours driving time? (3 marks)
  ii) How many people are within three hours of the Peak District National Park? Suggest **two** reasons for this high number. (3 marks)

Figure 13e

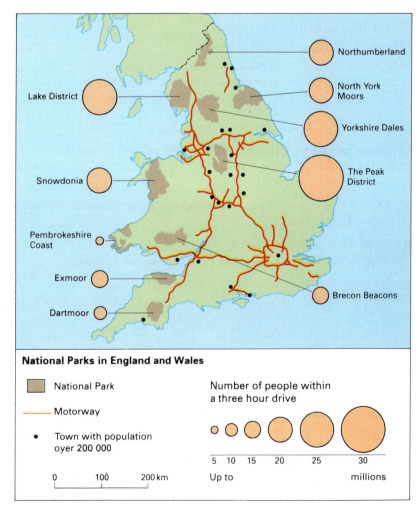

National Parks in England and Wales

Key: National Park, Motorway, Town with population over 200 000

Number of people within a three hour drive: Up to 5, 10, 15, 20, 25, 30 millions

COMPETITION FOR LAND

5 Refer to pages 110 and 111 in the resource book.
Study Figure 13f which shows land use in a part of the Peak District National Park.

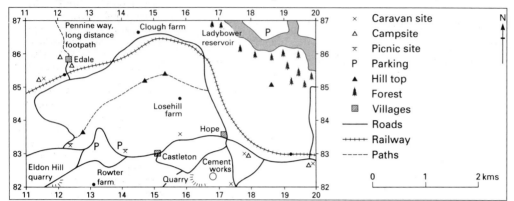

Figure 13f

a What is the distance in kilometres:
  i) from Castleton village (1582) to the cement works (1682),
      (1 mark)
  ii) from Castleton village (1582) to Ladybower reservoir (1886)?
      (1 mark)

b From the map give four tourist and four non-tourist land uses. Give a map reference for each, e.g. tourist-campsite-1285.
      (8 marks)

c Conflict often occurs between land uses in National Parks. Study Figure 13g which shows some conflict and some harmony between land uses.
  i) Copy and complete the matrix.   (4 marks)
  ii) Choose two of the land uses and in each case describe the conflicts likely to arise between tourists using the land for recreation and non-tourists earning their living in other ways.
      (4 marks)

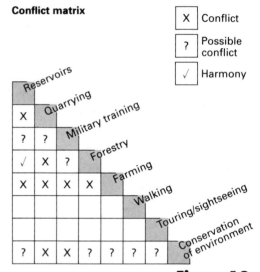

Figure 13g

6 Refer to pages 110 and 111 in the resource book.
Study the cartoon (Figure 13h) which shows some of the conflicts of interest which may arise in National Parks.

a Why are places with problems such as those shown in the cartoon sometimes called **honeypots**?   (2 marks)

b Describe the problems shown in the cartoon for each of the following:
  The local farmer, the tourist, the local resident.   (6 marks)

c Imagine you are a National Park Warden.
  Suggest what could be done to lessen the problem for those concerned.
      (6 marks)

Figure 13h

COMPETITION FOR LAND

7 Pages 110 and 111 of the resource book will help you to answer this question.

a Read the passage, which is based on a speech by Brian Redhead, President of the Council for National Parks.

What are the **two** duties of the National Park Authorities? For each of the duties give an example of the way in which National Park Authorities carry out that duty. (6 marks)

b Read the passage again.
  i) What reason does Brian Redhead give for stopping most forms of quarrying in National Parks? (2 marks)
  ii) Describe **two** disadvantages of quarrying in National Parks. (4 marks)
  iii) When the closure of a mine or quarry is proposed local residents often object. Give two reasons why local residents might object to such closures. (4 marks)

c i) National Parks are important tourist areas. Describe and explain one benefit and one problem that tourism has brought to National Parks. (6 marks)
  ii) Why are most National Parks in northern and western England and Wales? (3 marks)

> "The National Park Authorities have two principal duties to protect the natural beauty of the Parks and to ensure that the public has the access to enjoy them. What is quarrying but the authorised removal of a Park? Once you have dug out a chunk you cannot say that you are sorry and that you will put it back again. There should be no question of quarrying in the Parks for minerals that can be found elsewhere."

NEA, 2101 1989

---

8 Refer to page 111 in the resource book.

The building of new roads in national parks may bring both advantages and disadvantages.
Study Figure 13i which shows part of the Lake District National Park and two proposals to link the M6 and West Cumbria with a heavy lorry route.

a Give an advantage and a disadvantage of road development in National Parks. (2 marks)

b The Countryside Commission is a group concerned with protecting the countryside. This group supported the northern route. Suggest reasons for their choice. (2 marks)

c After a public enquiry the southern route was eventually chosen and is now in operation.

At the enquiry the following people and groups of people showed interest in the proposals and voiced their opinions.

**tourists   conservationists   industrial firms   local residents
farmers   shopkeepers**

Choose **four** of these and for each one chosen explain carefully how they would be affected by the road and what their attitudes towards it might be. (8 marks)

d Do you think that roads should be developed in National Parks? Give reasons for your answer. (4 marks)

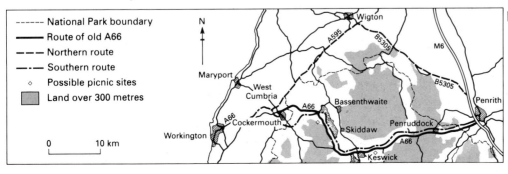

Figure 13i

FOURTEEN ENVIRONMENTAL ISSUES

1 Refer to Fig 14.1 on page 114 of the resource book which shows the causes and effects of acid rain.

a i) What are the **two** main causes of acid rain?
ii) Which **two** chemicals cause rain to be acid? (4 marks)

b i) Give **three** ways in which acid rain affects the natural environment.
ii) How can acid rain affect the 'built' (human) environment? (4 marks)

c i) How is the level of acidity in rain measured?
ii) At what level does rain become acid?
iii) At what level do fish die? (3 marks)

d i) Which part of Britain is most affected by acid rain?
ii) Give **one** reason why this area is the most affected. (2 marks)

2 Refer to page 115 in the resource book.

a i) Where is the ozone layer? (1 mark)
ii) Why is the ozone layer essential to humans? (1 mark)

b i) What are chlorofluorocarbons (CFCs)? (1 mark)
ii) Name **three** sources of CFCs in the atmosphere. (3 marks)
iii) Why are CFCs harmful to the environment? (1 mark)

c i) What can governments do to try to protect the ozone layer? (1 mark)
ii) Why is it difficult to get governments to work together to try to protect the ozone layer? (1 mark)

3 Refer to page 114 in the resource book.
The greenhouse effect is caused by the build up of gases in the atmosphere.

a Copy and complete the pie graph (Figure 14a) by:

i) Inserting the name of the **four** missing greenhouse gases.
ii) Naming **one** source for each of the **four** missing gases.
iii) Add colour to make the graph clearer and easier to read. (8 marks)

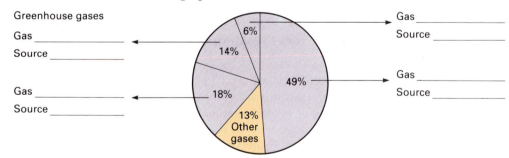

Figure 14a

b i) By how many degrees has the global temperature risen this century? (1 mark)
ii) By how many degrees are temperatures predicted to rise by the end of the next century? (1 mark)
iii) Why are global temperatures rising? (2 marks)

c Refer to Figure 14.2b on page 115 in the resource book.

i) List **four** advantages to Britain which are likely to result from the greenhouse effect.
ii) List **four** problems that will face Britain as a result of the greenhouse effect. (8 marks)

ENVIRONMENTAL ISSUES

4 Refer to page 118 in the resource book and use your own background knowledge. The landsketch (Figure 14b) shows several ways in which the environment may become polluted.

a By means of a list or a table, give **two** causes of each of the following types of pollution:
  i) air,
  ii) noise,
  iii) visual,
  iv) smell,
  v) water,
  vi) coastal. (12 marks)

b By means of a star (or explosion) diagram, list **three** of the actual causes of pollution which you consider to be the most damaging to the environment:
  i) at the present time,
  ii) for the future. (6 marks)

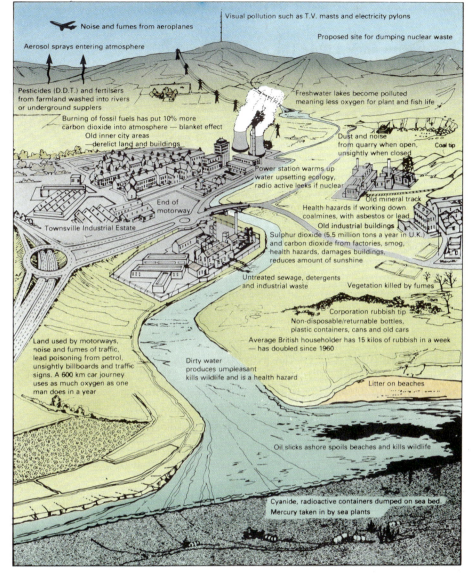

Figure 14b

5 Refer to pages 17, 26, 114-115 and 118-119 in the resource book. The eleven missing words in the crossword (Figure 14c) all refer to causes of pollution in our present day environment.

Figure 14c

1. The effect of raising world temperatures by releasing carbon dioxide into the atmosphere.
2. This kills fish and trees and destroys buildings.
3. The type of pollution which you can see.
4. Writing on walls of subways and buildings.
5. Car fumes pollute this.
6. Aerosols and CFCs are causing the thinning of this layer of the atmosphere.
7. The type of pollution experienced by living close to motorways and airports.
8. Fog with pollution in it.
9. A type of pollution left by tourists.
10. The most dangerous type of industrial waste.
11. These collect in rivers having been originally used as fertiliser by farmers. (11 marks)

FIFTEEN POLITICAL DECISIONS

1 Refer to page 122 in the resource book.
The Government has a policy of encouraging industrial growth in certain areas. Give **five** reasons for this policy. (5 marks)

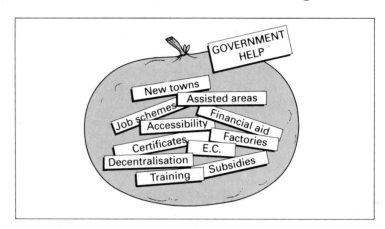

2 Refer to page 122 in the resource book.
Study Figure 15a which shows some types of help available to industry.

a To show how a government can help industry, write a sentence about any **six** of the types of help shown in the diagram. (12 marks)

b Which of the following areas have received government assistance since the early 1980s: Central Scotland, North-east Scotland, South Wales, Northern Ireland, North-east England, North west England, South-east England, East Anglia? (3 marks)

Figure 15a

GOVERNMENT HELP
New towns
Assisted areas
Job schemes
Accessibility
Financial aid
Factories
Certificates
E.C.
Decentralisation
Subsidies
Training

3 Refer to page 122 in the resource book.
Rather than providing direct help for industry, EC aid has been aimed at supporting industrial growth in areas needing assistance.
Study Figure 15b which shows some examples of EC aid.

a Describe and give the location of **three** projects that are linked to the supply of energy. (3 marks)

b Describe and give the location of **two** projects that help people improve their own chances in the job market. (2 marks)

c i) Give **three** examples of schemes that help improve accessibility. (3 marks)
ii) Describe how improved accessibility can affect the success of an industry? (2 marks)

Figure 15b

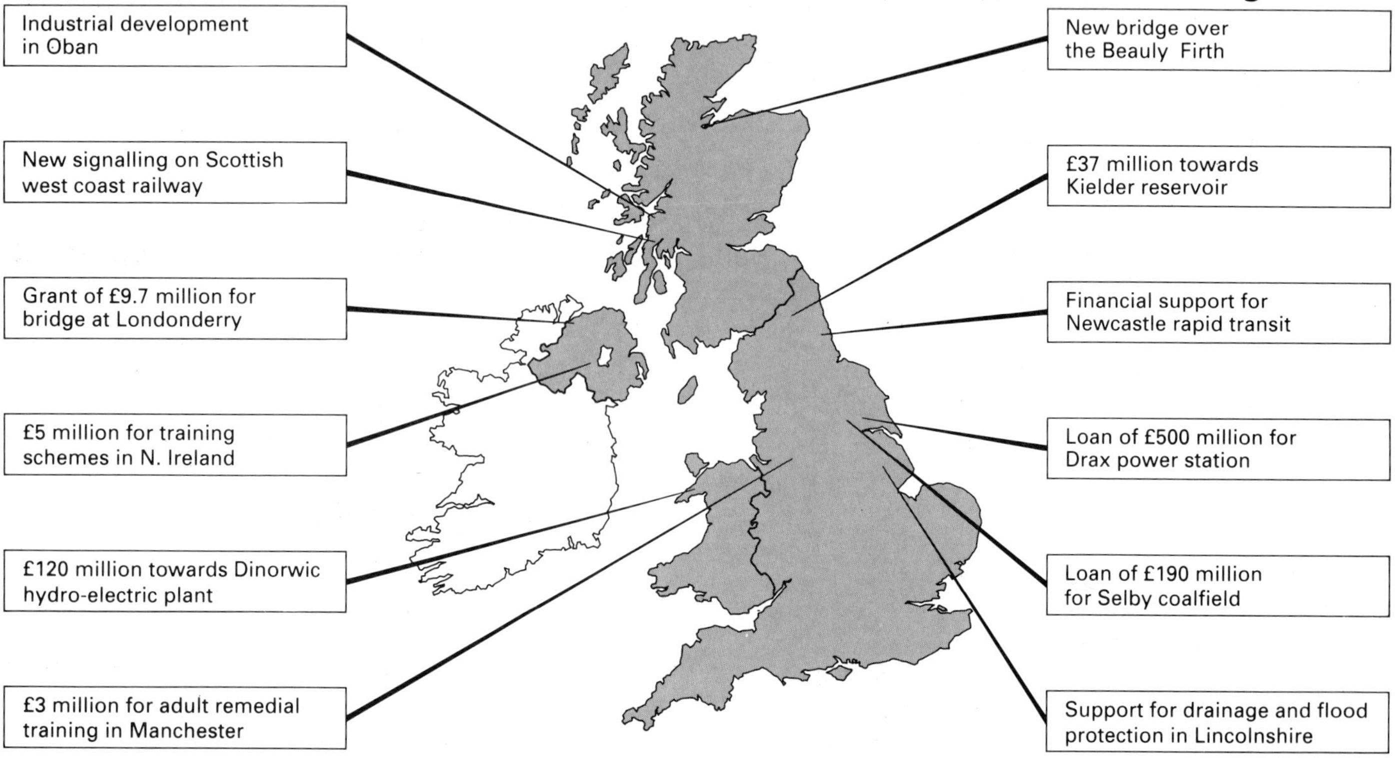

Industrial development in Oban
New signalling on Scottish west coast railway
Grant of £9.7 million for bridge at Londonderry
£5 million for training schemes in N. Ireland
£120 million towards Dinorwic hydro-electric plant
£3 million for adult remedial training in Manchester
New bridge over the Beauly Firth
£37 million towards Kielder reservoir
Financial support for Newcastle rapid transit
Loan of £500 million for Drax power station
Loan of £190 million for Selby coalfield
Support for drainage and flood protection in Lincolnshire

POLITICAL DECISIONS

4 Refer to pages 120 and 121 in the resource book.
a Why was the Highlands and Islands Development Board set up in 1965? (4 marks)

b i) Make a large copy of Figure 15c.
 ii) Describe the work of the Highlands and Islands Development Board by filling in the boxes.
    Write no more than 20 words in each box. Industry has been done to help you. (10 marks)

c What evidence is there to suggest that the HIDB has had some success in solving the problem of population decline? (2 marks)

Figure 15c

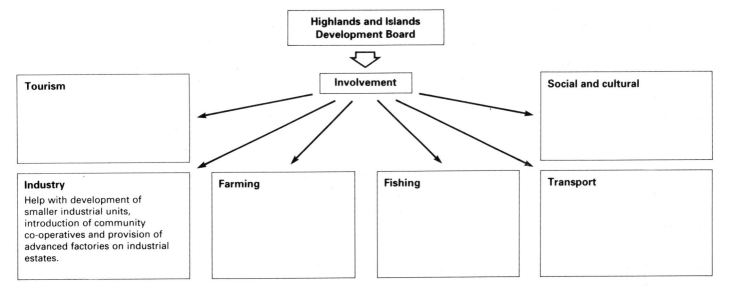

5 Refer to pages 124 and 125 in the resource book.
a i) What was the aim of Enterprise Zones when they were first introduced in 1981? (1 mark)
 ii) For which areas were Enterprise Zones planned? (1 mark)
 iii) Give **four** types of economic activity that are encouraged to develop in Enterprise Zones. (4 marks)
 iv) Name **five** of the original Enterprise Zones. (5 marks)

b Copy the star diagram in Figure 15d and complete it by adding some of the benefits available to industry in Enterprise Zones. (6 marks)

Figure 15d

c For the Clydeside Enterprise Zone or any other Enterprise Zone that you have studied, describe the main features by completing the following questions:
 i) Name the Zone and describe its location. (1 mark)
 ii) Describe the main features and problems of the area. (4 marks)
 iii) Describe what has been done to attract industry to the area. (2 marks)
 iv) Describe the successes of the area. (2 marks)
 v) Outline any problems that may have occurred. (2 marks)

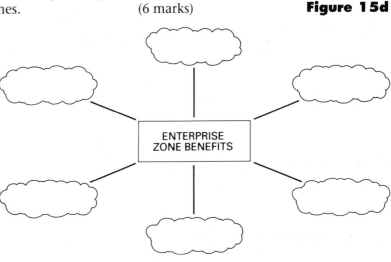

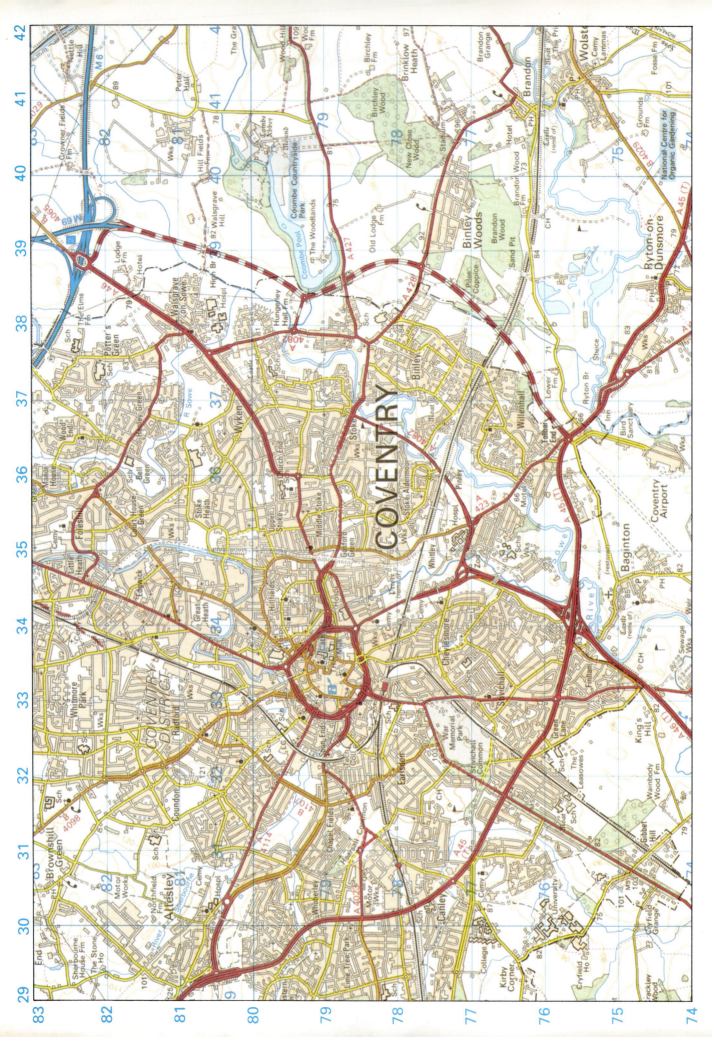

1:50 000 Second Series Map

CONVENTIONAL SIGNS

ROADS AND PATHS
Not necessarily rights of way

- Service area **M 1** Elevated — Motorway (dual carriageway)
- Junction number **18**
- Motorway under construction
- Unfenced · Footbridge — Trunk road
- Dual carriageway — Main road
- Main road under construction
- B 4114 — Secondary road
- A 855 · B 885 — Narrow road with passing places
- Bridge — Road generally more than 4 m wide
- Road generally less than 4 m wide
- Other road, drive or track
- Path
- Gradient: 1 in 5 and steeper   1 in 7 to 1 in 5
- Gates   Road tunnel
- Ferry P   Ferry V   Ferry (passenger)   Ferry (vehicle)

PUBLIC RIGHTS OF WAY
(Not applicable to Scotland)

- .... Footpath
- ———— Bridleway
- —·—·— Road used as a public path
- -+-+-+- Byway open to all traffic

Public rights of way indicated by these symbols have been derived from Definitive Maps as amended by later enactments or instruments held by Ordnance Survey on 1st April 1988 and are shown subject to the limitations imposed by the scale of mapping. Later information may be obtained from the appropriate County or London Borough Council.

The representation on this map of any other road, track or path is no evidence of the existence of a right of way

Danger Area   MOD Ranges in the area.   Danger!   Observe warning notices

WATER FEATURES

Marsh or salting, Towpath, Lock, Canal, Aqueduct, Weir, Bridge, Footbridge, Lake, Normal tidal limit, Ford, Slopes, Flat rock, Cliff, Sand, Dunes, Mud, High water mark, Low water mark, Lighthouse (in use), Lighthouse (disused), Beacon, Shingle, Canal (dry)

ABBREVIATIONS
- P   Post office
- PH   Public house
- MS   Milestone
- MP   Milepost
- CH   Clubhouse
- PC   Public convenience (in rural areas)
- TH   Town Hall, Guildhall or equivalent
- CG   Coastguard

ANTIQUITIES
- VILLA   Roman
- Castle   Non-Roman
- ⚔   Battlefield (with date)
- ☆   Tumulus
- +   Position of antiquity which cannot be drawn to scale
- ₥   Ancient Monuments and Historic Buildings in the care of the Secretaries of State for the Environment, for Scotland and for Wales and that are open to the public

The revision date of archaeological information varies over the sheet

TOURIST INFORMATION
- Information centre
- Parking
- Picnic site
- Viewpoint
- Camp site
- Caravan site
- Youth hostel
- Golf course or links
- Selected places of tourist interest
- Telephone, public/motoring organisation
- PC Public convenience (in rural areas)

RAILWAYS
- Track multiple or single
- Track narrow gauge
- Bridges, Footbridge
- Tunnel
- Viaduct
- Freight line, siding or tramway
- Station (a) principal (b) closed to passengers
- LC Level crossing
- Embankment
- Cutting

ROCK FEATURES
outcrop   cliff   scree

HEIGHTS
Contours are at 10 metres vertical interval   ·144 Heights are to the nearest metre above mean sea level

Heights shown close to a triangulation pillar refer to the station height at ground level and not necessarily to the summit.

GENERAL FEATURES
- Electricity transmission line (with pylons spaced conventionally)
- Pipe line (arrow indicates direction of flow)
- ruin Buildings
- Public buildings (selected)
- Bus or coach station
- Quarry
- Spoil heap, refuse tip or dump
- Coniferous wood
- Non-coniferous wood
- Mixed wood
- Orchard
- Park or ornamental grounds
- Radio or TV mast
- Church or Chapel { with tower / with spire / without tower or spire }
- Chimney or tower
- Glasshouse
- Graticule intersection at 5' intervals
- Heliport
- Triangulation pillar
- Windmill with or without sails
- Windpump

BOUNDARIES
- —+—+— National
- —·—·— County, Region or Islands Area
- —○—○— London Borough
- —·—·— District
- National Park or Forest Park
- NT National Trust   NT always open   NT opening restricted
- FC Forestry Commission   Pedestrians only -observe local signs

© Crown copyright

POLITICAL DECISION

6 Refer to pages 122 to 125 in the resource book.
Study Figure 15e which is part of an advertisement placed in a national newspaper to attract industry to Swansea Bay in South Wales.

Figure 15e

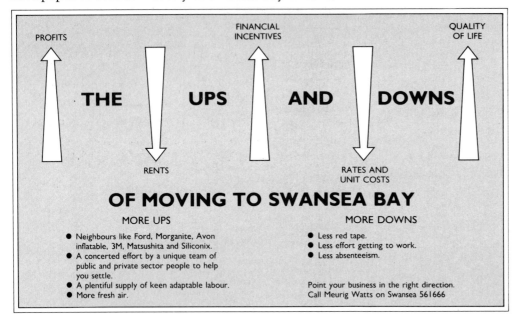

a Name **two** companies that are already located in Swansea Bay. (2 marks)

b Give **three** advantages of Swansea Bay as a place to set up industry. (3 marks)

c What is meant by the term 'quality of life'? (1 mark)

d Give **two** examples of financial incentives (advantages). (2 marks)

e What does the advertisement say about:
   i) the workforce, (1 mark)
   ii) help to get started? (1 mark)

f If you were an industrialist considering opening a new factory in Swansea Bay, explain how the factors in the advertisement might attract you to the area. (4 marks)

g What other factors would you investigate before choosing Swansea Bay as a location for your factory? (2 marks)

7 Refer to pages 120 to 125 in the resource book.
Imagine that you are a publicity officer for the Clydeside Enterprise zone or any other industrial area that is trying to attract new industries.
Design an advertisement for a national newspaper to attract new industry to your area.
Your advertisement should:

- have impact,
- be interesting, colourful and attractive,
- give the facts. (10 marks)

8 Refer to pages 120 to 125 in the resource book.
For a named area that you have studied, describe how the government (local or national) has influenced the nature of economic activity.
Your answer should be between a half and a full page in length. (10 marks)

POLITICAL DECISIONS

9 Refer to pages 122 to 125 in the resource book.
Study Figure 15f which gives information about Urban Development Corporations.

Figure 15f

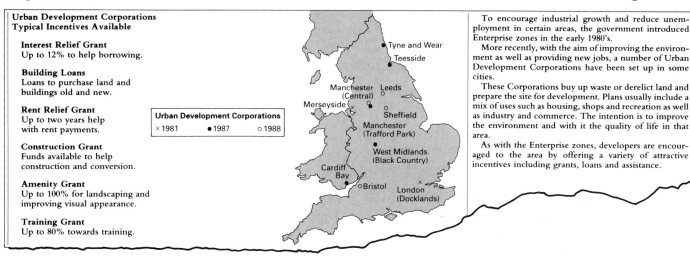

a i) What was the aim of Enterprise zones when they were first introduced in 1981? (2 marks)

ii) What are the aims of Urban Development Corporations (UDCs)? (2 marks)

iii) What is the meaning of the term 'environment'? (1 mark)

b i) By 1988 how many UDCs had been set up? (1 mark)

ii) Name the UDCs and give the date when each one was set up. (1 mark)

c i) Make a large copy of Figure 15g.

ii) Write the following statements in the correct boxes to show how a government through UDCs can affect the environment. (5 marks)

- Environment improved and new jobs and amenities made available.
- Government chooses area for 'clean-up' and development.
- Public funding and private investment secured.
- UDC obtains land, prepares site and draws up plans.
- Developers attracted to site through advertising and incentives.

iii) Give your diagram a suitable title. (1 mark)

Figure 15g

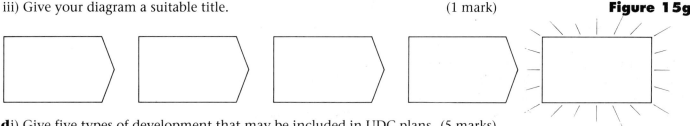

d i) Give five types of development that may be included in UDC plans. (5 marks)

ii) Draw a star diagram to show the benefits that may be available in UDC areas. (6 marks)

iii) Which incentive is designed to improve the environmental quality of any development? (1 mark)

e Imagine that you are a director of a company that owns several large shops and is considering opening new premises in a UDC area.
Write a report to your Board giving the advantages of the area for your company.
Your report should be no more than a page long and should include both financial and environmental factors. (10 marks)

SIXTEEN THE SEA

1 Refer to page 127 in the resource book.
Copy out and complete Figure 16a using the following:
large fish, mammals, plankton, small fish.
(4 marks)

2 Refer to page 126 in the resource book.
Match the type of sea pollution with the illness which it causes.

Cause of pollution	Illness
Mercury	Cancer
Lindane	Hepatitis and meningitis
Cadmium	Nervous disorders and paralysis
Untreated sewage	Brain and kidney damage
Lead	Kills dolphins. (5 marks)

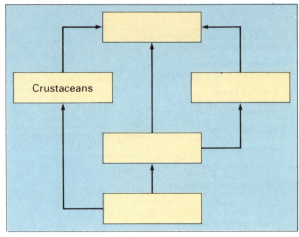

Figure 16a

3 Refer to pages 126 and 127 in the resource book and the fieldsketch (Figure 16b) showing part of Britain's coastline.

a How might features A to H cause pollution of the sea and beaches. (8 marks)

b What steps might the holiday resort at F take to try to win a Blue Flag Award? (3 marks)

4 Refer to page 127 in the resource book which describes the state of Britain's beaches.

a i) In which year did the EC set limits for the maximum level of pollution in waters used for bathing?
 ii) How many years were given for beaches and coastal waters to reach these accepted requirements? (2 marks)

b i) Describe **one** method used by English and Welsh Water Authorities to try to improve the cleanliness of the sea.
 ii) Why has this method not been successful at Southend? (4 marks)

c i) Give **five** requirements needed to gain a Blue Flag Beach Award? (5 marks)
 ii) How many British beaches gained this award in 1988? (1 mark)
 iii) Where are most of those beaches located? (1 mark)
 iv) Suggest two reasons why beaches with those locations described in iii) may be easier to keep clean. (2 marks)

Figure 16b

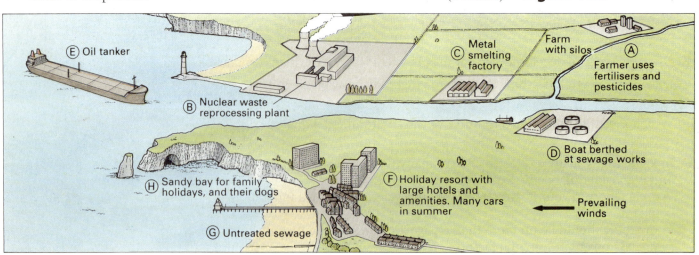